Winter

Lead Me in the Way Everlasting

VONETTE
Zachary
BRIGHT

NewLife
PUBLICATIONS

My Heart in His Hands:
Lead Me in the Way Everlasting

Published by
NewLife Publications
A ministry of Campus Crusade for Christ
P.O. Box 620877
Orlando, FL 32862-0877

Production by Genesis Group

Edited by Brenda Josee, Tammy Campbell, Joette Whims, and Lynn Copeland

Cover by Koechel Peterson Design

Printed in the United States of America

ISBN 1-56399-164-0

Unless otherwise indicated, Scripture quotations are from the *New International Version*, © 1973, 1978, 1984 by the International Bible Society. Published by Zondervan Bible Publishers, Grand Rapids, Michigan.

Scripture quotations designated NASB are from *The New American Standard Bible*, © 1960, 1962, 1963, 1968, 1971, 1972, 1973, 1975, 1977 by the Lockman Foundation, La Habra, California.

For more information, write:

Campus Crusade for Christ International—100 Lake Hart Drive, Orlando, FL 32832, USA

L.I.F.E., Campus Crusade for Christ—P.O. Box 40, Flemington Markets, 2129, Australia

Campus Crusade for Christ of Canada—Box 529, Sumas, WA 98295

Campus Crusade for Christ—Fairgate House, King's Road, Tyseley, Birmingham, B11 2AA, United Kingdom

Lay Institute for Evangelism, Campus Crusade for Christ— P.O. Box 8786, Auckland, 1035, New Zealand

Campus Crusade for Christ—9 Lock Road #3-03, PacCan Centre, Singapore

Great Commission Movement of Nigeria—P.O. Box 500, Jos, Plateau State, Nigeria, West Africa

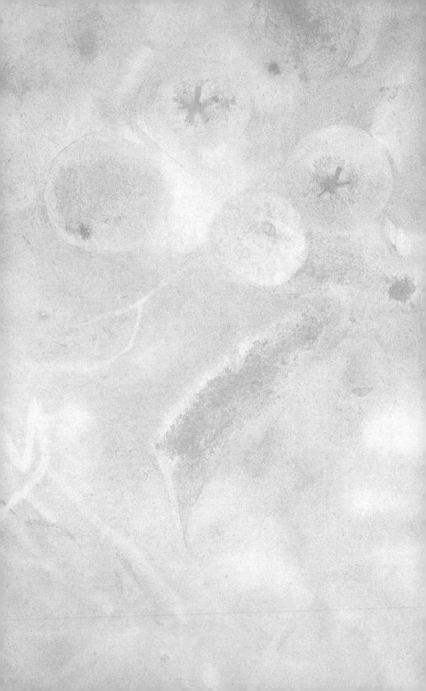

Contents

A Note of Thanks

I love being a woman. My mother made womanhood seem so special. She enjoyed working in the marketplace, but in no way deprived her family. I owe my visions of womanhood to her. My desire as a Christian woman has been not only to present the gospel to all who would listen, but to encourage women to be all they can be. They do this by finding their identity in Jesus Christ and their fulfillment in His plan for their life, then exerting their influence to improve the welfare of their home, community, nation, and the world.

I believe women largely hold the moral key to society. To mobilize them for the cause of Christ, Women Today International was created. Mary Graham, a twenty-seven-year Crusade staff member, co-directed this ministry, helped launch the radio program *Women Today with Vonette Bright*, and served as its producer. The scripts for these daily programs form the basis of this book—daily nuggets to help women find answers and encouragement, cope with circumstances, and realize their significance and influence.

To extend the ministry of the radio program was a dream of Brenda Josee. She is a good friend and a great encouragement to me. Her beautiful and creative ideas have made this book a reality. She and Tammy Campbell compiled, organized, and edited the scripts, and Joette Whims and Lynn Copeland gave the material a final edit. Michelle Treiber coordinated the cover design and printing. I also thank my dear husband, Bill, my greatest source of inspiration and encouragement, with whom I have enjoyed the adventure of trusting God for over fifty years.

My heartfelt thanks go to:

The current and former staff of *Women Today*—Judy Clark, Sallie Clingman, Pam Davis, Cherry Fields, Tina Hood, Liz Lazarian, JoAnn Lynch Licht, Robin Maroudi, Patty McClung, Kathy MacLeod, Judy Nelson, Anna Patterson, Laura Staudt Sherwood, Pam Sloop, Mary Ann White, Carrie Wright; the script writers—Christy Brain, Lisa Brockman, Rebecca Cotton, Angie Bruckner Grella, Keva Harrison, Kirsten Jarrett, Roger Kemp, Cindy Kinkaid, Tracy Lambert, Christi Mansfield, Linda Wall, Kara Austin Williams, Ann Wright; "The Committee" in Orlando; The Lighthouse Report; Ambassador Advertising; Evelyn Gibson; and Jim Sanders.

All of this to say, this book has been a gift to me from the hard work of others. I now present it to you. My prayer is that these devotionals will be an encouragement to you and will help you in a greater way to entrust *your heart into His hands*.

My dear friends,

The decision is now in the hands of the jury." We understand these familiar words.

"I will take matters into my own hands." Again, we know exactly what that means. Because we take hold of things physically with our hands, our hands symbolize control of situations, emotions, and ideas.

How many times have you asked someone, "Can you handle that?" There is One who is able to perfectly handle every aspect of your life. If you have accepted the Lord Jesus Christ as your Savior, the best way to describe the security of not only this life on earth, but also the eternal destiny of your soul, is to picture *your heart in the hands of God!*

The God who promised the descendants of Abraham, "I will uphold you with my righteous right hand" (Isaiah 41:10) also holds your heart in His hands.

Life is often hectic, and the responsibilities of women in our culture place enormous demands on our physical and emotional energy. By the time we meet the needs of the day, we may find little time to seek God's heart and find solace in the strength of His hands.

I love to see a mother cradle the head of her crying newborn in her hands and gently stroke away the tears.

The security that infant feels with the familiar touch of his mother calms him to sleep. That's the scene I picture when I come to God in prayer for my own needs and express my frustrations to Him. Just sitting quietly before Him, I can sense His gentle touch caressing my aching heart, and my burden is soon lifted.

King David said it so perfectly: "You open your hand and satisfy the desires of every living thing" (Psalm 145:16).

If you have not placed your heart in His hands, please do so today. You may have accepted the Lord Jesus as your Savior but are still struggling in your life because you don't know the security, comfort, and guidance of His hand. The psalmist assures you:

He who dwells in the shelter of the Most High
will rest in the shadow of the Almighty.
I will say of the LORD, "He is my refuge and my fortress,
my God, in whom I trust." (Psalm 91:1,2)

Give Him your whole heart and experience the peace and joy that will follow you through every season of your life.

From my joyful heart to yours,

Vonette Z. Bright

The Season for Contentment

Search me, O God, and know my heart;
test me and know my anxious thoughts.
See if there is any offensive way in me,
and lead me in the way everlasting.

PSALM 139:23,24

It has been said, "A picture is worth a thousand words." Paint this picture in your mind: a New England countryside, complete with white steepled church and snow-roofed cottages with smoke curling from chimneys. A peek inside reveals a crackling fire and a table set for breakfast with hot muffins and cocoa. It didn't take a thousand words to create an image that evokes an *ahhhh* from most women. This pleasant scene depicts true contentment.

The reality behind the serene winter scene is quickly overlooked; seldom is a thought given to the hard work of shoveling snow on the entrance to the cottage or of chopping firewood to create the warm fire. Though not real, the mental picture briefly satisfies the longing we have in our hearts for true contentment.

But we have a better reality available to us. God has promised us true contentment. By placing our hearts in His hands, we can live through the cold winter seasons of grief, disappointment, and frustration and still know a deep, settled peace.

These winter seasons are necessary for the balance of creation. The purification of the soil in the dormant cold months yields a beautiful harvest in the months ahead.

Every woman faces winter seasons in her emotional and spiritual life. If you are experiencing a dormant or chilly season, remember God's promise to "never leave you nor forsake you" (Hebrews 3:15). You can trust His faithfulness, and if you will fill your mind with His Word, your heart can rest content.

Applying the words of Scripture to our life allows us to always have a heart focused on God, balanced emotions, a lifestyle of purity, and the confidence that He is leading us "in the way everlasting."

The devotional readings in this book are written to encourage you to examine your heart and life, and to recognize the ways that God has worked in the lives of others.

The Guided Heart

Whatever you do, work at it with all your heart, as working for the Lord, not men.

COLOSSIANS 3:23

Most of the hours of our day are spent on "maintenance" requirements—doing things that must be done again the very next day. If we are not careful, we can spend the majority of our life maintaining and never pressing forward to expand our minds and broaden our scope of influence.

Women have a wonderful ability to balance many tasks and to patiently work toward the completion of long-term goals. That is the very essence of a life strategy. Paul described his life in Philippians 3:14: "I press on toward the goal to win the prize for which God has called me heavenward in Christ Jesus." I encourage you to prayerfully ask God to guide you as you develop a strategy for your life. Spend time in His Word, and after prayerful consideration, write out a strategy. You will find that it defines the purpose for your future activities. It will then be easy to determine how many activities in your day support or detract from your life strategy.

Having self-imposed goals without a strategy may bring you frustration and a sense of defeat, but having a life strategy allows for various detours and interruptions, providing a base of confidence that the goal is still in view.

Be certain to base your strategy on a Christ-centered lifestyle that will bring glory and honor to your heavenly Father.

DAY 1

Florence Chadwick was a seasoned long-distance swimmer who, in 1952, set out to swim the channel between Catalina Island and the California coast. She had many obstacles to overcome that July day. The shark-infested water was incredibly cold. The fog was so thick she could barely see the boats alongside her.

Don't Give Up!

After fifteen long, grueling hours, she felt as though she could swim no longer. Her muscles screamed with pain and she was totally exhausted.

Her coach, of course, pleaded with her to keep going. "It's just a little farther. You're almost there! Don't give up!"

But when Florence looked ahead, all she could see was a blanket of fog. Tired, cold, and totally discouraged, Florence quit. She quit! Florence had a goal, but her view was clouded. She couldn't see the shoreline.

Have you ever strived to reach a goal only to quit because your view became clouded with unimportant issues, difficulties, or sin? As Christians, our ultimate goal is to follow Christ. Hebrews 12:2 advises us, "Let us fix our eyes on Jesus, the author and perfecter of our faith."

If we fix our eyes on Him, we will reach His goal for our life.

What Florence didn't know when she quit was that the shoreline was a mere half mile away.

Two months after her first attempt, Florence tried the swim again. This time, she not only made it, but also set a new speed record! What made the difference? The shoreline had not moved closer. The water was still very cold. But this time, the sky was blue, and Florence could see land!

Dear friend, like Florence, we can lose heart when we lose sight of our Guide, our end-marker. Fix your eyes on Jesus, and you will finish the race no matter what obstacles you encounter.

HIS WORD
"You need to persevere so that when you have done the will of God, you will receive what he has promised" (Hebrews 10:36).

MY PART
"Lord Jesus, when the fog rolls into my life, help me to keep my eyes fixed on You. Your light is a beacon in the darkness, guiding me home. With You leading me, I will complete the race. In Your matchless name, amen."

MY STUDY
Psalm 141:8–10; Isaiah 2:5

DAY 2

"**H**ow do I know God's will?" You may have asked that very question. Here are a few guidelines for helping you to determine God's will.

How Do I Know?

First, God's will for your life will *never* run contrary to His Word. For instance, the Bible says you shouldn't lie. So if you find yourself with a job opportunity where you are asked to lie, that job isn't God's will. He'll *never* require you to do something that is in direct conflict with what is spelled out in Scripture.

Second, pray for God to show you His will. Be specific. God answers prayer, but first we have to ask Him. Then, listen for His response—perhaps not in an audible voice, but in the gentle leading of the Holy Spirit.

Third, let me encourage you to not sit idly by waiting for the clouds to roll back and God's voice to speak to you directly. An old saying goes, "It's easier to steer a moving vehicle." Take practical, logical steps to determine God's will: talk with friends; ask questions of those who know you; look for input from those who have been in a similar situation.

Then lastly, when seeking God's will, remember that His plan for you is not confusing, but crystal clear. Let me assure you, if the answer is not obvious, then you may be headed in the wrong direction.

The apostle Paul encourages us through his letter to the Corinthian church, "God is not a God of disorder, but of peace" (1 Corinthians 14:33).

If God hasn't given you peace or your decision is not absolutely clear, then *wait!*

Dear friend, God will always be faithful to show you His will. But it's important to remember: His timing is perfect. Although we may be thinking we need to know right now, His purpose might be fulfilled only after a delay. Trust Him!

HIS WORD
"Teach me to do your will, for you are my God; may your good Spirit lead me on level ground" (Psalm 143:10).

MY PART
Are you struggling to determine God's will on a particular issue in your life? First pray, asking God for guidance. Then follow the steps laid out in today's devotion. God promises that if you seek Him, He will be found. God is faithful. You can trust Him to always keep His promises.

MY STUDY
1 Kings 22:5; John 12:26

As a young girl, Sandra dreamed of studying English or psychology and pursuing a related career. But Sandra's graduation was placed on hold when she married Bob and gave birth to their first son.

His Perfect Timing

Investing in her children gave her great satisfaction. Her family was her first priority, but Sandra never allowed her dream to die.

A few years later, Sandra and Bob became full-time missionaries with Campus Crusade for Christ. With their four young sons, they moved to Kenya, East Africa. In Kenya, Sandra was asked to teach a six-week class on parenting, providing practical information on building a healthy home. The participants enjoyed the class so much that she agreed to teach it three times a year.

This class gave Sandra a platform to cultivate her gifts and underscored her need for professional training. Her childhood dream of obtaining a degree in psychology was rekindled.

After eleven years in Kenya, Sandra and Bob felt God calling them back to the U.S. With her youngest son in high school, Sandra had the freedom to finish college and get her master's degree. Now Sandra works full-time in counseling missionaries, conducting team-building workshops, and interviewing prospective missionaries. She's living out her childhood dream!

Do you have any dreams on hold? You may be at home, investing in your family. Let me urge you to stay at this all-important task. At the same time, don't be tempted to believe your dream has died. Life is a journey, and often God takes us on the scenic route before we reach the "promised land."

Sandra says that by obeying God's calling, she has had a far more exciting and satisfying life than if she'd merely set out to accomplish her own goals.

My friend, God has some great adventures for you if you are willing to listen to His call, go wherever He leads, and wait for His perfect timing.

HIS WORD
"Wait for the LORD; be strong and take heart and wait for the LORD" (Psalm 27:14).

MY PART
Whatever you're doing today—if you're in school, if you're a mother, if you're developing a career—make yourself available to the Lord. Follow His leading. He will use your interests and abilities, and in His timing will take you places you never dreamed possible.

MY STUDY
Isaiah 30:18; Hebrews 6:13–15

DAY 4

Nancy was programmed to succeed. She'd been a nationally ranked swimmer, graduated *cum laude*, and become a company executive. She was co-authoring a book and dating a wonderful man. From the outside, her life was going extremely well. But inside, she was deeply dissatisfied.

Tell Your Story

She and her colleagues went out almost every night to drink and brag about their achievements. But back home in the stillness of the night, Nancy knew that she wasn't that wonderful. The "happy hours" didn't make her very "happy." She wondered if she'd ever find true contentment.

Sensing the problem had something to do with a spiritual void, she visited church occasionally, went to retreats, read lots of books, and prayed. But nothing seemed to work.

Then one Sunday, she attended a church where people shared stories of how the Lord had changed their lives. Strangely attracted to this group, she came back the next Sunday and the next. As Nancy listened week after week, she realized these people had truly found joy and fulfillment. She wanted *desperately* to be like them.

So Nancy took a class at the church on how to write a personal testimony. She thought that once she wrote out her story, she'd be able to see how God had changed her life, too.

The instructor read Nancy's detailed autobiography and said, "This is quite a confession. But when did you receive Jesus as your Savior and Lord?"

Nancy was floored by this question. It had never occurred to her that a Savior and Lord was available to her, but that very night, she received Christ. She was flooded with a sense of God's peace—what she'd been hungry for all her life. It felt like coming home.

My friend, no worldly accomplishment will satisfy the longing in your heart. Only experiencing God's love and forgiveness can fill that void. Walking daily with His Spirit will sustain your joy.

HIS WORD
"He says, 'In the time of my favor I heard you, and in the day of salvation I helped you.' I tell you, now is the time of God's favor, now is the day of salvation" (2 Corinthians 6:2).

MY PART
When sharing Christ with others, don't judge whether or not they'll be ready to accept Him. Remember, it's God who prepares hearts so they're ready to receive Him. All you have to do is tell your story. Write your testimony and be prepared to share it when the occasion arises.

MY STUDY
Psalm 18:6; Isaiah 45:22

Joanne, an American college student, went on a short-term evangelistic mission trip to Kenya. When she arrived, Joanne was assigned to help a Kenyan family—not as an evangelist, but as a housekeeper.

The Servant

At first Joanne accepted her chores—doing the laundry, cooking, and dishes—without complaining. She bided her time, waiting for the "real" ministry of evangelism to start.

By the second week, she began to get angry. As she did the laundry, she thought, *I didn't come all this way to get a degree in housekeeping! I'm better than this! They just want me to be their servant.*

Suddenly, she remembered Philippians 2:5,6: "Your attitude should be the same as that of Jesus Christ: Who…did not consider equality with God something to be grasped, but made Himself nothing, taking the very nature of a servant."

Clearly, she saw that doing the family's laundry was being like Jesus. *That* was her mission.

The work around the house didn't change, but Joanne changed. She relaxed into the role God had given her, not to be an evangelist, but to serve the family as best she could.

A week after Joanne's return to America, she overheard some Kenyan students talking about their mission trip. They knew what had happened to Joanne. Her time as a housekeeper in their homeland had made quite an impression on them. Her attitude and willingness to serve made the Christian message even more attractive.

As a result, the following summer, Kenyan students joined with the American students for an evangelistic outreach. Hundreds came to Christ and the students worked together because of the unprecedented fact that an American girl had served as a housekeeper in a Kenyan home.

My friend, to be a person of real influence, we must learn to be a servant of all. We are called to imitate Jesus Christ—the ultimate Servant.

HIS WORD
"When pride comes, then comes disgrace, but with humility comes wisdom" (Proverbs 11:2).

MY PART
"Lord Jesus, Your willingness to humble Yourself to become a servant of men is truly an example to me. You place great value on humility. Help me to be a humble servant to those around me. In Your holy name, amen."

MY STUDY
Zephaniah 2:3; Luke 1:46–49

Do you ever lie awake at night and think about your greatest dream? The thing you'd like most to achieve?

Big Dreams

Dreams and goals are wonderful. We all should have a few. I believe God gives each person talents, abilities, likes, and dislikes. God places on our hearts goals, aspirations, and ideas that drive us to attempt great achievements for Him.

I'm not promoting worldly success. But what I am encouraging you to do is to pursue your dreams. Dream big dreams. Ponder big thoughts for God. Believe Him for the goal, for the dream. Then take the steps needed to make your dream come true. Persevere. Keep on going. Don't give up.

At one time or another, all of us have had to face discouragement and rejection. It can feel like the end of the world. At those times, never forget that God cares deeply about you. And He promises to never leave your side. Joshua 1:9 says, "Be strong and courageous. Do not be terrified; do not be discouraged, for the LORD your God will be with you wherever you go."

Your dream may be to go to school to get an advanced degree. Perhaps you'd like to get your family out of debt and begin giving greater sums to charitable concerns. Maybe your dream is to share the gospel with one person each week.

Whatever it is, with God's strength you *can* do it. And whatever it is, you can use it to touch the lives of others.

Don't be surprised when you see your dream come true. God is a God of His Word. He will accomplish it through you and will allow your life to make a difference!

My friend, don't settle for little dreams. Fulfill the purpose God has planned for you! You will be able to accomplish great things through God's Spirit.

HIS WORD

"The LORD will fulfill his purpose for me; your love, O LORD, endures forever— do not abandon the works of your hands" (Psalm 138:8).

MY PART

Choose to be strong and courageous today. Make time today to write a brief statement about your dream. Write out Joshua 1:9 at the very top of the paper. Then choose one thing you can do today to start fulfilling that dream.

MY STUDY

Job 17:9; Colossians 1:10–12

Louie Giglio's dad was a gifted commercial artist. On one occasion, his father came home with a gigantic piece he called the "Abstract Magician." More than nine feet tall and almost four feet wide, it was a looming, gruesome figure with a bow tie, cape, and colored scarf.

The Big Picture

Louie's mom hated it, and she wasn't thrilled when he hung it at the top of the staircase for all to see. Graciously, Louie's dad modified the "Abstract Magician" by lopping off a huge chunk from the bottom of the picture. He put this smaller and nicer rendition back on the wall.

A few years later, Louie's father was struck with a near-fatal brain virus, leaving him physically and mentally disabled. It kept him from doing any more artwork.

Many years later, Louie found the part of the painting that had been lopped off. He hung this discarded piece in his office.

Louie says he has people come into his office all the

time who declare, "That's the ugliest thing I've ever seen!" His quick response is, "That's because you can't see the whole thing. When I look at it, I never see this small painting. I see the whole guy, all nine feet of him. And I think about my father, the artist."

Louie's point is that life is a series of snapshots, a series of paintings that are halfway finished, or a series of paintings that have been re-framed. Humans can't see the whole thing. But God always sees the entire canvas. It may not be until heaven that we finally say, "Now…now it makes sense!"

Have you become so engrossed with a little corner of the canvas you've lost sight of the big picture?

God wants to use you. And He has a plan—a big, beautiful piece of art bearing your likeness. Take heart, dear friend! You can trust God with your snapshots. He *always* sees the big picture.

HIS WORD

"We are God's workmanship, created in Christ Jesus to do good works, which God prepared in advance for us to do" (Ephesians 2:10).

MY PART

God has not given us the whole picture of our lives because He wants us to trust Him. Whatever you are facing today, know that the God who loves you sees the whole picture. In fact, He created the picture.

MY STUDY

Genesis 5:1,2; Psalm 22:9,10

DAY 8

In 1903, with a little experience in dairy products, a young man moved to Chicago to start a business. If he could put his cheese-making theories to work, he knew he would turn a profit. To get started, he bought cheese from a manufacturer to sell.

The Partner

He arrived in Chicago with $65 in his pocket. He bought a cart and rented a horse. He and Paddy, the horse, worked very hard.

By the end of the first year, however, he was $3,000 in debt. Soon he could no longer get credit to buy cheese. He kept trying and working harder, but still had no success.

Then one day, determined to sell $100 worth, he loaded the cart full of cheese. At the end of the long, hard day, he counted his money: $12.65. That's all he'd made.

Can you imagine the disappointment he must have felt? He and Paddy walked sadly toward home. Dejectedly, he wondered aloud, "What's the matter with me anyhow?" Just then, he thought, *I'm working without God rather than with Him!* So right then and there, He made God his business partner.

I'm sure you're familiar with this man's business. He's J. L. Kraft, the founder of the Kraft Cheese Company! And I don't have to tell you how God blessed his business—*after* he made God his partner.

My friend, when you make God a partner in your life, He'll bless you more than you can imagine. It may not be in dollars, but it will be in personal satisfaction, meaning, and purpose.

No matter what your business is—whether you're an interior decorator, a stay-at-home mom, a lawyer, a sales clerk, or a teacher—God wants to be your partner.

Paul told the Philippians, "I can do everything through him who gives me strength" (4:13).

When you allow God to give direction to your life, you *can* do all things.

HIS WORD
"Blessed is the man who makes the LORD his trust, who does not look to the proud, to those who turn aside to false gods" (Psalm 40:4).

MY PART
In your work, what do you want to accomplish? What are some of your goals? Write those down on paper. Put today's date on it. Then begin praying right now for God to show you what to do and how to do it. Then start doing it!

MY STUDY
Isaiah 26:4;
1 Timothy 6:20,21

Steve was a wrestler on his high school varsity team. After school, he would put on two sweat suits for a strenuous work out. The students were required to do fifty pushups without stopping. If even one person faltered, the whole team had to start over. Even if they'd done forty-nine pushups, they had to start over.

Lasting Rewards

Then the coach would make the wrestlers run up and down stairs twenty-five times. Finally, they would wrestle as though they were in a real match. To top it all off, after practice Steve would run home.

For dinner the night before a match, Steve drank skim milk and ate very lean meat. The next day, he'd head straight for the scales. If he were even an ounce over 119 pounds, he'd be required to suck on a lemon and spit all day in an effort to rid himself of that ounce.

Steve did all that for one reason—he wanted to earn a letter jacket. That jacket was Steve's reward!

First Corinthians 9:25 says, "Everyone who competes in the games goes into strict training. They do it to get a crown that will not last."

Today, I'm sure Steve has no attachment to that jacket.

The verse goes on to say, "But we [who follow Christ] do [our work] to get a crown that will last forever." This "imperishable" crown will never tarnish, fade, or lose its value.

Every day, you and I are motivated by rewards. Most of the rewards don't last. There's only one thing we can do that lasts, and it's tied to our relationship with Jesus Christ. We can trust and obey Him.

If that's your desire, dear friend, no matter what you do today, you'll be investing in eternity. And when you see Him face to face, you'll receive the greatest and most lasting of all rewards: His pleasure in you. You'll hear Him say to you, "Well done, My good and faithful servant."

HIS WORD

"The nations will see your righteousness, and all kings your glory; you will be called by a new name that the mouth of the LORD will bestow. You will be a crown of splendor in the LORD's hand, a royal diadem in the hand of your God" (Isaiah 62:2,3).

MY PART

What do you need to do today? Care for a child? Meet a deadline at work? Share your faith? Pray, "Lord, You know that I need your help. You've promised in Your Word to work through me. Help me trust You and be obedient to all You've called me to do today."

MY STUDY

Psalm 19:9–11; James 1:12

DAY 10

William Borden was born into a family of great wealth and was heir to the family's fortune.

After graduating from high school, he traveled abroad. During this time, God impressed it upon his heart to give his life to missions.

No Regrets

While William was in college, his father died. His family asked him to take over the family business. But William was committed to following God's direction. He wrote on the flyleaf of his Bible, "No Reserve." And without reservation he continued preparing for the mission field.

Later, he finished seminary studies. His friends encouraged him to stay in America and to become a pastor. But no, God had called him to go. On the flyleaf of his Bible, he added this: "No Retreat." And with that he never looked back.

Soon he was on his way to Cairo, Egypt. Four months into his mission service, he became ill. William Borden died. His body, with his Bible resting on his chest, was shipped back to Chicago.

As his brokenhearted family looked through his

Bible, they found one more inscription, written the day before William died. He wrote these words: "No Regrets."

William's story influenced thousands of young people to get involved in the Student Volunteer Movement. They gave their lives to taking the message of God's love to the world. There's never been anything quite like it since.

William Borden could have commanded a fortune. But it's unlikely his wealth could have influenced more people for the cause of Christ. It was his character, his commitment to God, and God's call on his life that touched so many lives. He set an example others could follow. And they did.

Friend, whatever God calls you to do, do it. Don't ever give up. Be one of the few like William Borden. Be committed. Write his words in the cover of your Bible: "No Reserve. No Retreat." You will have "No Regrets."

HIS WORD

"Jesus said to them, '. . . Everyone who has left houses or brothers or sisters or father or mother or children or fields for my sake will receive a hundred times as much and will inherit eternal life'" (Matthew 19:28,29).

MY PART

"Faithful Lord Jesus, You have said that You will never leave me nor forsake me. Because of this constant assurance, I can follow You with my whole heart, mind, soul, and strength. You are worthy of my complete allegiance. In Your mighty name, amen."

MY STUDY
1 Samuel 3:7–10; Psalm 57:7

Thelma Wells had just graduated from high school and was ambitious about her future as a secretary. After calling the secretarial school for registration information, she excitedly put on her new blue dress and rode a bus to the school.

God's Way

Enthusiastically, Thelma burst through the school door. Within minutes, she was on her way back out. When the admissions officer saw her face to face, he refused to let her enroll. She met all the qualifications for the school except for one detail. Thelma is black, and in the early sixties, this particular school was open only to white students.

Crushed and humiliated, Thelma went home. As she told her great-grandmother, she cried. Her great-grandmother was understanding and encouraging. "Oh, honey," she said, "don't worry. God will make a way."

Later, her grandmother, who worked as a housekeeper, mentioned the situation to her employer. The employer had compassion on Thelma. "Thelma," she said, "I want to pay your tuition and expenses for college. I require only two things. You must keep your grades above a C average, and you mustn't marry until you finish school."

So Thelma Wells, with her dream to attend a two-year secretarial school, became the recipient of a much greater gift—a four-year college education—and became the first in her family to earn a college degree. God made a way—and His way was much better.

Today, Thelma is an author and motivational/inspirational speaker. She tells her story all over the country, imparting hope and faith to those who struggle with disappointment. God knew the plans He had for Thelma Wells. His plan was even greater than she'd imagined.

Discrimination is sinful, and God hates sin. But He is not limited by it! How I rejoice that He sovereignly provided for Thelma in spite of sin. Dear friend, He will sovereignly provide for you. He has a plan.

HIS WORD

"In this hope we were saved. But hope that is seen is no hope at all. Who hopes for what he already has? But if we hope for what we do not yet have, we wait for it patiently" (Romans 8:24,25).

MY PART

Does someone or something seem to be holding you back today? Are you discouraged because the disobedience or sin of another seems to be a barrier to the fulfillment of your dream? Don't be dismayed. God can work through any circumstance and most likely has a better plan.

MY STUDY

2 Samuel 7:9–11; Psalm 111:4–6

DAY 12

Many Christians desire marriage, but God has called some to a life of singleness. Listen to what Crusade staff member Nancy Wilson says about being single.

Undivided Devotion

People ask Nancy why she's not married. Her answer? It's not God's will. She has come to look at her singleness as a gift, and God's Word teaches that every good and perfect gift comes from Him. "Singleness may not be one of the spiritual gifts listed by the apostle Paul in his letters," Nancy says. "But he certainly treated his own singleness as a gift. In 1 Corinthians 7:8, he says: 'Now to the unmarried and the widows I say: It is good for them to stay unmarried, as I am.'"

Many years ago, Nancy thought she'd met her Prince Charming. After she told God all the reasons why this man was the one for her, she sensed God's reply: *But Nancy, how much more can you glorify Me if I teach you how to live with an unfulfilled desire?* Understandably, she didn't want to hear that. But through her tears she said, "Father, I want Your will more than mine. Take away anything that's not Your will for me." God took away not only that relationship, but others.

Singleness is a calling to a deeper love relationship with Jesus, to undivided devotion to Him. It is also a calling to love others as He loves us—unselfishly, generously, and universally.

Nancy says, "If you're single, take time to talk with God, to embrace His gift of singleness to you and offer it back to Him so He may sanctify it for His purposes."

We can be honest with God about anything, including emotions about singleness. Though Nancy has struggled at times, her perspective on her singleness is encouraging and godly.

Dear friends, single or married, if you focus on your relationship with Christ, you will live a life of contentment and will glorify God.

HIS WORD

"An unmarried woman or virgin is concerned about the Lord's affairs: Her aim is to be devoted to the Lord in both body and spirit" (1 Corinthians 7:34).

MY PART

If you're single, talk with God about any struggle you have and seek to embrace your singleness as a perfect gift from Him. Only God knows tomorrow, but today, God has called you to be single. Say yes to the fullness God has for you.

MY STUDY

Psalm 63:2–4; Isaiah 26:9

Ten years ago, Amy began a life-long friendship with God. She heard someone speak about Abraham being God's friend, and Amy decided she wanted to be God's friend, too. So she put her faith in Christ. Her commitment to God changed her earthly friendships forever.

The Model Friend

Over the years, Amy has been taught a few truths about friendship, especially friendships with other believers. She learned that friends are also a wonderful source of love and encouragement. First Thessalonians 5:11 says, "Therefore encourage one another and build each other up." Here are a few other lessons she learned.

First, Christian friendships can be a safe place to be real and accepted. Friends refine us by keeping us accountable to each other. Proverbs 27:17 tells us, "As iron sharpens iron, so one man sharpens another." And in Proverbs 17:17, we read, "A friend loves at all times, and a brother is born for adversity."

Second, in friendships we learn about forgiveness. Colossians 3:13 tells us, "Bear with each other and forgive whatever grievances you may have against one another. Forgive as the Lord forgave you." God commands us to forgive one another. I have found that the more I forgive, the more I understand Christ's love and forgiveness of me.

Third, we learn to work through conflict. The Bible tells us that before we offer our gift at the altar, we must "first go and be reconciled to your brother; then come and offer your gift" (Matthew 5:24). God wants us to live in peace. It is a priority for Him. He knows that we will have conflict, but He wants us to practice the kind of humility with each other that will bring about reconciliation.

From her friendship with God, Amy has learned invaluable lessons about being the kind of friend He wants her to be. When you're a friend of God, He will help you be a better friend to others. Let Him be your guide.

HIS WORD

"Whatever you have learned or received or heard from me, or seen in me—put it into practice. And the God of peace will be with you" (Philippians 4:9).

MY PART

"Lord, thank You for my friends. Help me to exhibit the Christlike qualities of a good friend that You have demonstrated to us. Help me to be loving, encouraging, accepting, forgiving, and humble. I need the strength of Your Spirit. In Your matchless name, amen."

MY STUDY

Ruth 1:16,17; Psalm 133:1

What would you like others to notice about you? Your eyes? Your smile? Perhaps your answer to this question would be the same as Sara's, a Campus Crusade for Christ staff member.

Gentleness

She looks to the qualities described in 1 Peter 3:4, which says that a gentle and quiet spirit is of "great worth in God's sight." A gentle and quiet spirit is characterized by peace. Being a peaceful person is the opposite of being an overwhelming, overpowering, and dominating person. It is the opposite of demanding your own way.

The world tells women of today that we need to be strong by taking charge of a situation and by not being dominated by anyone. The world views as weakness the gentleness and quietness described in the Bible. But God's Word tells us these qualities are precisely what we should strive to exhibit.

Philippians 4:5 says, "Let your gentleness be evident to all. The Lord is near." Gentleness is an exterior quality that will be seen clearly by others.

What does it mean to be gentle? *Baker's Evangelical*

Dictionary defines "gentleness" this way: "Sensitivity of disposition and kindness of behavior, founded on strength and prompted by love."

Gentleness should not only be part of our personality or disposition, it should be an act of our will, a behavior. "Be completely humble and gentle; be patient, bearing with one another in love" (Ephesians 4:2).

Sara prays that nonbelievers will notice these imperishable qualities in her—and then be drawn to the Lord because of it. She says, "I want my life to radiate the sweetness and love of God."

My friend, we should all seek to radiate the sweetness and love of God. Pray for a gentle and quiet spirit and ask God to help you display these qualities before others. Then watch God weave them into your life.

HIS WORD

"The fruit of right-eousness will be peace; the effect of righteousness will be quietness and confidence forever" (Isaiah 32:17).

MY PART

In which situations do you find the most difficulty in exhibiting a gentle spirit? Seek ways to calm your spirit when you start to feel irritated or impatient. Ask God for assistance during these times. Let His Spirit fill you with gentleness and peace in dealing with difficult circumstances.

MY STUDY
*Psalm 131:2;
James 3:17,18*

DAY 15

Psychologist Neil Clark Warren asked a chronically discontent woman what would make her happy. She said, "A better job with better pay, a better boss, a better marriage—and a two-week vacation to Maui."

Rejoice!

Dr. Warren believes many of us are also unfulfilled, empty, and discontent. He says: "Contentment has everything to do with what's going on inside [of us]. Show me a person who is happy because she is vacationing on Maui, and I'll show you a person who has only a few days to be happy. But show me a person who has learned to cultivate deep-down contentment, and I'll show you a consistently contented person."

Friend, contentment is cultivated in and through God and His Word. Paul speaks to us about contentment in Philippians 4:11,12: "I am not saying this because I am in need, for I have learned to be content whatever the circumstances. I know what it is to be in need, and I know what it is to have plenty. I have learned the secret of being content in any and every situation, whether well fed or hungry, whether living in plenty or in want."

Paul learned the secret of being content. What is this secret? We can look a few verses earlier for evidence of what the "secret" is. In verse 4 Paul tells us, "Rejoice in the Lord always. I will say it again: Rejoice!" Does this verse say we should rejoice only when things are going well? No. It says we should rejoice always, even when things aren't going well and we are experiencing pain.

Contentment doesn't happen automatically. It takes an act of the will to decide to respond to life in a godly manner. If we can learn to "rejoice in the Lord always," we will be cultivating a life of "deep-down contentment." We will be spreading God's secret to living abundantly.

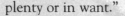

HIS WORD

"May all who seek you rejoice and be glad in you; may those who love your salvation always say, 'The LORD be exalted!'" (Psalm 40:16).

MY PART

In life, we all encounter situations or circumstances that are not what we would choose for ourselves, and we can end up feeling discontent. Make it a daily practice to cover any discontentment with rejoicing in the Lord. Then contentment will come.

MY STUDY
Deuteronomy 12:7;
Acts 2:25–28

Where do you work? Perhaps in an office, at a construction site, or at home with your children. No matter where we are, we all have work to do.

A Good Thing

God created work all the way back in the beginning. In Genesis 2:15 we are told, "The LORD God took the man and put him in the Garden of Eden to work it and take care of it." So, work is a good thing. We were meant to labor and take care of what God has given us.

The *New Geneva Study Bible* explains the concept of work this way: "Man was to find fulfillment, not in idleness, but in a life of rewarding labor in obedience to God's command."

God mandated work to make our lives full and meaningful. Have you ever been sick at home, unable to do your normal activities? If you are like I am, you tend to feel restless, like there is more you should be doing. That drive to be productive with our time was put there by God. It is this drive that enables us to provide for our families, fulfill our dreams, and accomplish the tasks God sets before us.

God did not say that the work would be easy, but He did give us a guideline about how we should do whatever work we are doing. In Colossians, we're told this: "Whatever you do, work at it with all your heart, as working for the Lord, not for men" (3:23).

Dear friend, although we work to fulfill earthly needs, we should not work to please men. But we should work to bring honor and glory to God, who is the Creator of work. When we work this way, we will feel a deeper sense of fulfillment and purpose. As you look at your daily life from this perspective, my prayer is that it will renew your strength as you labor for the God who loves you.

HIS WORD

"Blessed are all who fear the LORD, who walk in his ways. You will eat the fruit of your labor; blessings and prosperity will be yours" (Psalm 128:1,2).

MY PART

"Heavenly Father, thank You for providing me with a means to earn a living, but also a place to use the talents You have given me. Help me to make all that I do pleasing in Your sight and fruitful for Your kingdom. In Jesus' name, amen."

MY STUDY

Exodus 35:30–35; 1 Thessalonians 4:11

I like Thelma Wells' description of a bumblebee. She tells about the insect at the Outrageous Joy conferences, a conference for women held around the United States.

Bumblebees

Thelma says that, aerodynamically speaking, bumblebees shouldn't be able to fly. Their bodies are too heavy for their narrow wing span. But the bumblebee doesn't know it can't fly. And it doesn't lie in bed asking, "Should I fly?" No, the bumblebee just flies, doing what God intended for it to do.

Unlike the bumblebee, we as humans often get blinded by our own inadequacies. Our finite minds get caught up in analyzing why we can't do something. We tell ourselves that we don't have a certain talent or ability. We tell God that He is asking the impossible of us. Then we never get around to doing what God has intended for us to do.

God does not assign tasks to us because of our strength. He assigns them based on *His* strength. The Bible gives us an encouraging word in Philippians 4:13: "I can do everything through him who gives me strength." God alone is our source of strength.

Where we are weak, He is strong. Paul tells us in 2 Corinthians 12:9, "He said to me, 'My grace is sufficient for you, for my power is made perfect in weakness.' Therefore I will boast all the more gladly about my weaknesses, so that Christ's power may rest on me." In fact, it is when we are weak and accomplish great things in His power that we bring the greatest glory to His name.

Dear friend, take it from the bumblebee: Don't spend your energy worrying about what you can and cannot do. God made you, so He knows where you are weak. Just follow where He leads and trust that whatever He asks you to do, He will give you the strength to do it. Then give the glory for your accomplishments to Him.

HIS WORD

"Proclaim the power of God, whose majesty is over Israel, whose power is in the skies. You are awesome, O God, in your sanctuary; the God of Israel gives power and strength to his people. Praise be to God!" (Psalm 68:34,35).

MY PART

What is God asking you to do right now? Is it something you feel completely inadequate to do? That's good. God wants you to know that, apart from Him, you can do nothing. He is the Source of your strength. Ask Him to work through you each day.

MY STUDY

Judges 6:14–16; Colossians 1:10–12

We all have goals that we want to accomplish. God-given goals are not a bad thing. God wants us to have goals, targets to strive toward. But even if we have a goal or target, what God really wants from us is to allow Him to guide our steps, day by day.

Step by Step

When I have deadlines to meet on a large project, I'm tempted to procrastinate. The task before me can seem to be overwhelming, and at times, I have no idea where I should start.

One way to keep from procrastinating is to set daily and weekly goals for yourself. These step-by-step markers can keep you from becoming intimidated by a large task, which is often the reason we procrastinate. It is in these individual steps that God wishes to guide us.

Proverbs 16:9 tells us, "In his heart a man plans his course, but the LORD determines his steps." With God's help, we can plan the general direction of our lives, but God also wants to be with us each day leading and directing us with His Holy Spirit. In other words, He sets the course, then He enables us to get to the goal.

Having a schedule or a step-by-step guide is good in

that it keeps us disciplined and focused, but I never want to be an inflexible slave to my schedule. I want to be open to the leading of the Holy Spirit so that I can accomplish all that God has called me to do and to be. If He changes my course, I want to fall right in line with His plan.

Friend, what has God called you to do and be today? Do you have a game plan for accomplishing that? Remember, God is with you each step of the way and wants to enable you to accomplish the challenging tasks He has assigned to you. Trust Him, today and every day.

HIS WORD

"I know, O LORD, that a man's life is not his own; it is not for man to direct his steps" (Jeremiah 10:23).

MY PART

"Almighty God, thank You that You give me goals to strive toward. But thank You most of all that You do not expect me to get there by myself. You are with me every step of the way. In Your Son's faithful name, amen."

MY STUDY

Proverbs 12:5; John 16:12–14

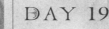

Have you ever wondered how God really wants you to serve? First, you need a willing spirit.

Read Lynne's story. Fresh out of college, she eagerly told God, "Use me, Lord!" And He did—as a young wife.

The Body

Later, Lynne again prayed, "Use me, Lord!" He did —to change diapers and to serve her young family.

When the children were in school, she cried again, "Use me, Lord!" He did—to drive carpools and volunteer.

God did not use Lynne to blaze trails the way she had thought He would. But He used her as an effective servant: as a godly wife and loving mother. These are both very important and exalted roles.

In 1 Corinthians 12, we read about God's plan for us all to have different roles. "The body is a unit, though it is made up of many parts; and though all its parts are many, they form one body. So it is with Christ. For we were all baptized by one Spirit into one body...God has arranged the parts in the body, every one of them, just as he wanted them to be. If they were all one part, where would the body be? As it is, there are many parts, but one body" (vv. 12,13,18–20).

We are all different parts of the Body of Christ, the worldwide church. Each of us has a valuable function. Some functions are more public than others. But whether you have a public function like a mouth or a hand, or you have a private function like a heart or an appendix, each part is important to the complete functioning of the body.

My friend, wherever you are in your life, pray Lynne's prayer, "Use me, Lord!" Then rest assured that He will use you in the function for which He designed you, and be content knowing that you are fulfilling the purpose He has for you.

HIS WORD

"Just as each of us has one body with many members, and these members do not all have the same function, so in Christ we who are many form one body, and each member belongs to all the others" (Romans 12:4,5).

MY PART

What part of the body are you right now? Whatever part that is, rest assured that God has a unique purpose for you. No one else is just like you, so no one else can function in the body like you can. Thank God for His wisdom in placing you exactly where you need to be.

MY STUDY

Psalm 138:8; Isaiah 41:10

DAY 20

As a teen-age hemophiliac, Steve Sawyer contracted the AIDS virus through a blood transfusion. A few years later, while in college, Steve placed his trust in Christ.

Follow Me

"I know I've been given heaven. So what am I going to do about it?" he once said.

This is what he did: He dropped out of college and began traveling worldwide, speaking to more than 100,000 students about Jesus Christ. Some 10,000 accepted Christ as their Savior.

Steve died in 1999 at age 24. His short lifetime is an example to us of what it means to "take up our cross and follow Christ."

As a Christian, you, too, have been given heaven. But the one-time act of salvation does not mean that you go back to living for yourself. You are not your own anymore. You belong to Christ, and He expects complete devotion.

The phrase "follow me" is used throughout the Gospels in the New Testament. In Luke 9:23,24, Jesus said to His disciples: "If anyone would come after me, he must deny himself and take up his cross daily and follow me. For whoever wants to save his life will lose it, but whoever loses his life for me will save it."

To be a true follower of Christ, we must die to our own desires each day and follow the path that He lays out for us. The amazing, heavenly logic of God's plan is that when we lose our life in this way, we will actually be saving it.

Dear friend, perhaps you are not facing a life-or-death situation like Steve Sawyer was, but we can all learn from his example. Don't wait for tomorrow to begin living your life completely sold-out to God, dead to yourself. As Jesus said, "Whoever loses his life for me will save it."

HIS WORD

"I wait for your salvation, O LORD, and I follow your commands" (Psalm 119:166).

MY PART

Are you completely dead to yourself? Do you submit your will to Christ daily? Begin each morning by asking God to use you and work through you. Give up your own rights that His will may be done. Throughout the day, remind yourself through prayer whose life you are living.

MY STUDY

Deuteronomy 13:4; Matthew 10:37–39

DAY 21

Dealing with uncertainty and the unexpected can be difficult. Most people like stability, and they like to see their plans work out.

Under Control

Gary learned on an overseas mission trip *not* to expect his plans to work out. In a foreign country, too many variables left holes in his plans. But as each hole occurred, he watched God, in His sovereignty, fill in the gaps. And when God worked, He always exceeded Gary's expectations.

Gary looks at variables differently now. Whenever plans don't go as expected, Gary trusts God to work in a different way.

Gary said, "Rather than be discouraged or frustrated because my plans didn't happen, this trip helped me learn to trust God more. My plans don't have to work out for God's work to be accomplished."

We read in Proverbs 19:21, "Many are the plans in a man's heart, but it is the LORD's purpose that prevails." We can make plans. It's part of leading a disciplined, productive life. But we need to realize that God is in control. When our plans don't work as we want them to, we can trust that God's plans will be better for us and enable Him to receive the glory.

Friend, God is working for your good. The familiar verse in Romans reassures us of this: "We know that in all things God works for the good of those who love him, who have been called according to his purpose" (8:28). He is working in everything that happens in your life—good and bad, expected and unexpected—to teach you, to bless you, to stretch you, to lead you.

Exceed your own expectations. Seek God's will in your planning. Make Him the focus of your plans and the center of your dreams. Then know that even when life doesn't go as you intended or expected, you can trust that our all-knowing God has it all under control.

HIS WORD
"The foolishness of God is wiser than man's wisdom, and the weakness of God is stronger than man's strength" (1 Corinthians 1:25).

MY PART
"Almighty God, You want what is best for me. I will trust that Your sovereign power will work everything to my benefit. Help me to let go of trying to control the world around me, which only leads to worry and disappointment. I trust You, Lord. Amen."

MY STUDY
Job 37:14–16; Psalm 18:31–33

Ambition is defined as "an eager or strong desire to achieve something." Although ambition can be a positive trait, the Bible gives us evidence that it can be considered a negative trait. Numerous times in the New Testament, believers are warned against "selfish ambition." This is ambition that seeks to satisfy one's own desires above those of God or even the best interests of the people around you.

Ambition

In Philippians 2:3 we read, "Do nothing out of selfish ambition or vain conceit, but in humility consider others better than yourselves." Be watchful of your motives. It is always better to act with humility and concern for others.

Dr. Ted Engstrom, the leader of Youth for Christ and World Vision for almost four decades, believes ambition is a positive trait when it is done under the guidance of the Holy Spirit. Dr. Engstrom says, "I asked the Lord, in the midst of strong ambition, to make sure that I understood what His will was for my life. God said He'd guide me with His eye—I leaned heavily on that."

He was referring to Psalm 32:8, in which God says:

"I will instruct you and teach you in the way you should go; I will counsel you and watch over you." Dr. Engstrom is talking about ambition that is in line with God's will.

Paul was himself ambitious, and in Romans 15:20, we are told the reason for his ambition: "It has always been my ambition to preach the gospel where Christ was not known." Paul's desire to spread the good news of Christ was a godly ambition.

Dear friend, God has given us ambition to keep us striving toward new goals. But this drive is subject to the leadership of Christ. Be ambitious for God. Seek Him first and ask Him to watch over you and guide you. Strive to let all you do bring Him glory. That's godly ambition!

HIS WORD
"'Therefore I will teach them—this time I will teach them my power and might. Then they will know that my name is the LORD'" (Jeremiah 16:21).

MY PART
What are your ambitions? Is there a goal you would like to achieve? First, ask God and search the Scriptures to determine if this goal is godly. Then, allow the Holy Spirit to guide you as you move step by step toward your goal.

MY STUDY
Psalm 119:66;
1 Timothy 4:8–11

DAY 23

Facing a deadline, Ginger was tremendously burdened by the pressure to complete her task on time.

His Strength

As she prayed, she remembered Psalm 138:8, which says, "The Lord will accomplish what concerns me" (NASB). The *New International Version* of the Bible translates the verse this way: "The Lord will fulfill his purpose for me."

In the midst of her preoccupation, Ginger prayed just the opposite. She prayed that *she* would accomplish what concerned God. She said, "It revealed the attitude of my heart. I was doing everything in my own strength."

Immediately, she confessed her self-sufficient attitude to God, and she asked Him to accomplish His purpose through her. As a result, she didn't feel so overwhelmed. She knew God was helping her to finish the project.

All of us feel overwhelmed at times. Perhaps it is a large project you are working on or maybe it's just the daily demands on your time and energy from family, friends, work, and church. When that happens, we need

to stop and ask ourselves, "Am I working under my own strength or am I allowing God to work through me?" If you are feeling burdened, you are probably working on your own.

Jesus addressed this issue in Matthew 11 when He said, "Come to me, all you who are weary and burdened, and I will give you rest … For my yoke is easy and my burden is light" (vv. 28,30). When we learn to rest in the Lord's strength, the burdens will lift and we will feel at rest.

Friend, don't try to live each day on your own or confine God to certain areas of your life. That is relying on your own self-sufficiency. Instead, in all that you do, allow God to work through you. He will give you the strength that you need to accomplish His purposes for you.

HIS WORD

"Blessed is she who has believed that what the Lord has said to her will be accomplished!" (Luke 1:45).

MY PART

"Lord Jesus, when I am overwhelmed, I only need to come to You, lay my burdens at Your feet, and rest assured that You are in control. By giving You control, I will receive peace. Please accomplish Your purposes through me. Amen."

MY STUDY

2 Kings 19:31; Psalm 81:6,7

DAY 24

What does it mean to be faithful? *Webster's Dictionary* defines "faithful" this way: "Firm in adherence to promises or in observance of duty." God has demonstrated His faithfulness to us through His adherence to His promises. The Bible tells us in Deuteronomy 7:9, "Know therefore that the LORD your God is God; he is the faithful God, keeping his covenant of love to a thousand generations of those who love him and keep his commands."

Stand Firm

Throughout history, Christians have demonstrated faithfulness to Christ and His Great Commission to bring others to a saving knowledge of Him. Their acts of faithfulness have been felt generations later.

In the 1800s, one obscure Sunday school teacher helped lead D. L. Moody to faith. In turn, Moody influenced thousands through his own ministry.

Joseph Stowell, president of Moody Bible Institute, wrote: "Even Billy Graham's conversion can be traced to a succession of converts that extends from D. L. Moody... God has far more in mind for us than simple faithfulness for today. He uses our commitment to His cause to set the stage for things greater than we could dream of, far beyond the borders of our lives."

Faithfulness is the characteristic that produces a many-fold blessing. Jesus said in Luke 16:10, "Whoever can be trusted with very little can also be trusted with much, and whoever is dishonest with very little will also be dishonest with much." As we prove ourselves faithful in our daily duties, God will give us increasing amounts of challenges and responsibilities for His kingdom. But rest assured, we are only responsible for our faithfulness. God is responsible for the results.

Dear friend, always be faithful to the cause of Christ! Even during times of discouragement or pain, keep your focus on what you know God wants you to do. God will bless you and bring about wonderful results.

HIS WORD
"The LORD rewards every man for his righteousness and faithfulness" (1 Samuel 26:23).

MY PART
Are you having difficulty being diligent in the tasks before you? Perhaps you don't see the results of your labor, but believe that God is using your obedience. Ask God to help you stand firm in your faithfulness.

MY STUDY
Proverbs 3:3; Matthew 24:45–47

DAY 25

World-class consulting firms, Fortune 500 companies, family empires. These are the plans of Harvard Business School's best graduates.

Choices

Steve, a Christian, earned top honors at the Massachusetts Institute of Technology (MIT). But while working toward an MBA at Harvard University, he became keenly aware of the emptiness of worldly success.

As the last speaker at a banquet with his peers, Steve told of his plans after graduation. He said, "I'm joining the staff of Campus Crusade for Christ." Silence filled the room. Graduating from the mecca of capitalism only to work for a nonprofit organization was unheard of.

This gentleman is Steve Douglass. Today, he is the newly inducted president of Campus Crusade for Christ. His ministry of more than thirty years has influenced thousands for Christ.

In Luke 16, Jesus says, "No servant can serve two masters. Either he will hate the one and love the other, or he will be devoted to the one and despise the other. You cannot serve both God and Money" (v. 13). Steve had a choice. He could let his life be led by the pursuit of material wealth, which he very likely would have gained, or he could let his life be led by His Master, which held no guarantee of material wealth but guaranteed peace and satisfaction. Steve chose the latter.

What choice have you made? What is your greatest priority? When we are making decisions in life, we often face two distinct paths. One is the path of worldly riches and accolades. The other is the path of heavenly riches and eternal life. One will provide temporary fulfillment and the other will bless with abundant life.

Oh, friend, reconsider the value of wealth and worldly success. In whatever you do, choose today to serve Christ. Someday you will hear Christ say, "Well done, good and faithful servant!"

HIS WORD

"His master replied, 'Well done, good and faithful servant! You have been faithful with a few things; I will put you in charge of many things. Come and share your master's happiness!'" (Matthew 25:21).

MY PART

"Almighty God, You are the Great Provider. You will sustain all my needs. Help me to choose the path of righteousness in all that I do. May Your Holy Spirit guide me and direct me. In Your Son's holy name, amen."

MY STUDY

Psalm 73:24; Isaiah 58:11

DAY 26

In high school, Tom told Diana he wanted to be a missionary. She thought it was a dream he would outgrow.

But in college, Tom continued to talk about missions. Diana began to recognize that God chose Tom for mission work. She also believed Tom was the man God would have her marry. So, she trusted God to work out the details.

At the end of seminary, Diana was asked about her call to missions. She answered honestly when she said, "I don't have a particular call to be a missionary. My call is being Tom's wife."

Diane has expressed a biblical view of marriage and the wife's role in it. Ephesians 5:23,24 says, "For the husband is the head of the wife as Christ is the head of the church, his body, of which he is the Savior. Now as the church submits to Christ, so also wives should submit to their husbands in everything."

Man is the head of the family as Christ is the head of the Church. God ordained that position. Although a wife may not have the same vision the husband does,

God's role for her is to be a helper and supporter. If God is calling the husband to a certain area, rest assured that He is concerned about the entire family. If you will recognize God's leadership and submit to it, you'll find that He will change your heart to match that of your husband's. He will give you the heart to respond. He did that for me.

God wants a husband and wife to be unified, first in their devotion to Christ, next in their devotion to each other. Dear friend, put Christ first in your marriage, then you will see your family unit moving in the same direction—toward God's will. As you all move in the same direction, you will find that your differences and conflicts will be easier to resolve in God's power.

HIS WORD
"I want you to realize that the head of every man is Christ, and the head of the woman is man, and the head of Christ is God" (1 Corinthians 11:3).

MY PART
Is your family facing a tough decision, perhaps one in which you and your husband have differing opinions? Make sure your husband understands your opinion. But in any relationship, someone must make a final decision. God holds him responsible for that decision. And if the decision differs from your opinion, voluntarily submit, asking God to give you the heart to respond.

MY STUDY
*Genesis 2:24;
Proverbs 19:14*

Have you ever desired to be physically different than you are? Is there some part of your body that you wish had been created differently? Before you answer these questions, read Amy's story.

Brown Eyes

Amy, a young Irish girl, desperately wanted blue eyes. One night she prayed for blue eyes, then confidently went to bed. When she awoke, she ran to the mirror. She was disappointed to still see her very brown eyes.

Years later, Amy Carmichael was a missionary to India. While there, she learned of young girls from poor families being sold as prostitutes. Courageously, she rescued them by staining her skin with coffee grounds and dressing in Indian garb.

What was the key reason this disguise worked? Amy had brown eyes! If her eyes had been blue, she couldn't have passed for an Indian woman. God gave her brown eyes so she could save hundreds of innocent girls!

Psalm 139:13–16 is a wonderful passage of Scripture telling about God's great care in creating each one of us and telling of His infinite knowledge of our lives. The passage says:

> You created my inmost being; you knit me together in my mother's womb. I praise you because I am fearfully and wonderfully made; your works are wonderful, I know that full well. My frame was not hidden from you when I was made in the secret place. When I was woven together in the depths of the earth, your eyes saw my unformed body. All the days ordained for me were written in your book before one of them came to be.

My friend, God "knit you together" the way He did for His very specific purpose. Your age, your size, the color of your skin and eyes. None of these attributes happened by chance. God was not only deliberate in His creation of your body, He is deliberate about the course of your life. Put Your trust in His care, each day.

HIS WORD

"The LORD God formed the man from the dust of the ground and breathed into his nostrils the breath of life, and the man became a living being" (Genesis 2:7).

MY PART

"Great Creator God, thank You for Your thoughtfulness in creating every part of me. Help me to take good care of this vessel You have given me, but also help me to appreciate how I am different from others. You want to use me in a unique way. In Jesus' name, amen."

MY STUDY

Psalm 103:13,14; Matthew 10:29–31

DAY 28

Maybe you've heard this saying: There is no limit to what God can do with a woman's life if she doesn't care who gets the credit. What quality does this saying describe? The biblical virtue of humility.

Life of Humility

When we happen across a great idea or when we execute a plan with success, it's easy to become proud of our achievements. Perhaps we want affirmation or praise from others for who we are and what we have done. This is not an unusual human desire. But, as believers, God is in control of our lives. All the credit for successes or achievements should go to Him. He created us and He is in control of every circumstance in our lives. He gave us various talents, abilities, and strengths, and He provides the opportunities for us to use them. Therefore, humility, not pride, should mark our lives.

James 3:13 says, "Who is wise and understanding among you? Let him show it by his good life, by deeds done in the humility that comes from wisdom." Deeds done with humility show the presence of wisdom in a person.

In Proverbs we read about where wisdom comes from: "The fear of the LORD teaches a man wisdom, and humility comes before honor" (15:33).

So let's look at the progression. Fear (or reverence) for God teaches wisdom, and wisdom leads to humility. Then, in God's timing and for His purposes, honor will come your way. Perhaps it will be earthly honor, but rest assured there will be heavenly honor.

One thing is very clear: you can't find genuine humility on your own. God will provide it to a reverent heart, yielded to Him. And you will find, dear friend, there truly is no limit to what God can do with a woman's life if she doesn't care who gets the credit.

HIS WORD
"Submit to one another out of reverence for Christ" (Ephesians 5:21).

MY PART
Practice reverence for God in the following ways: Seek His counsel through prayer on matters great and small. Under the power of the Holy Spirit, speak out against the sin around you. Give God the glory and praise for all the blessings He has given you.

MY STUDY
Proverbs 11:2; Daniel 6:26

DAY 29

There are certain things money can't buy. Things like love, contentment, or a child.

Empty Arms

As a young girl, Stephanie played with dolls, fantasizing about being a mom. When she and David married, it never occurred to her that they might have trouble becoming parents. But after several years, many medical tests, and numerous doctor visits, they were still unable to have a baby.

Stephanie says, "You would think that after many years I'd be used to a monthly disappointment, but the grief and pain never cease. I've read numerous books, all of which assure me that I'm not alone. Still, sometimes I feel like I *am* all alone in the struggle.

"At times I just want God to send me a telegram:

Dear Stephanie,
At this time I've decided not to give you children.
You can quit bugging Me about it.
   Love,
   God"

Stephanie knows that God doesn't work that way. So she continues to pray, wait, and hope.

She says, "I have no guarantees that God will ever allow us to have children of our own, or that we'll ever be able to adopt. But this I know—He loves us. Our empty arms long to be filled with a child, but we must trust God to fill them with Himself instead."

Stephanie has learned that God can meet her need, and she's learned to wait on Him. In her relationship with Him, she's found contentment.

True satisfaction can come only from an intimate relationship with God. Times of need can help show us God's heart and help us trust Him more. There's no better place to begin learning than in His Word. Some have called it His love letter to His children.

I know the pain of disappointment. I know the frustration of waiting. And I know, too, the deep satisfaction that comes only from God. Let Him fill your empty arms today with His love.

HIS WORD

"I will make an everlasting covenant with them: I will never stop doing good to them, and I will inspire them to fear me, so that they will never turn away from me. I will rejoice in doing them good and will assuredly plant them in this land with all my heart and soul" (Jeremiah 32:40,41).

MY PART

Are you experiencing disappointment? God is there to comfort you. Spend time with Him in prayer. Share your heart with Him and let His Words comfort you. Allow His Spirit to minister to you and your disappointment will begin to fade away.

MY STUDY

Proverbs 8:34,35; Philippians 2:1,2

Astronauts gain a perspective of earth very few people will have. As a little girl, Wendy Lawrence stared up at the stars and dreamed about being an astronaut and orbiting the earth.

Dream Big

From an early age, she was surrounded by people who dreamed big dreams. Her father was in the Navy and had come very close to joining the seven Mercury astronauts. John Glenn was a family friend.

Even though her friends insisted she was chasing a fantasy, Wendy went to work—excelling in high school and then joining the U.S. Navy.

Wendy pursued her master's degree at MIT. There she became involved with Campus Crusade for Christ, personally discipled by a Crusade staff member. She participated in Bible studies and attended several conferences. Her relationship with God was her number one priority—even during a hectic training schedule.

Finally, on March 2, 1995, she climbed aboard the space shuttle Endeavor with six other astronauts at the Johnson Space Center. Her role was Mission Specialist One—Flight Engineer. The mission was a complete success, and it fulfilled a lifelong dream of someone who was told it couldn't be done.

As a young woman, Wendy committed her life to Christ and walked faithfully with Him. And she had a goal, a dream few women would dare to dream. She took her aspirations seriously and went to work. It required intense training —both physically and mentally.

As a result, a woman of Christian character represents our nation as an accomplished astronaut. When she's not on a space mission, she's accomplishing another mission —one she considers even more important: reaching others for Christ.

Someone asked Wendy about going into space and she responded, "While it's a wonderful adventure, there's no greater adventure than walking with God."

Having watched the earth spin in space from the shuttle—as few people have, or ever will—that's quite a statement. We serve a mighty God!

HIS WORD

"'I am the Alpha and the Omega,' says the Lord God, 'who is, and who was, and who is to come, the Almighty'" (Revelation 1:8).

MY PART

Do you have a dream today? Are there mountains you'd like to climb? Goals to achieve? Has God placed a burden on your heart? Go for it! We desperately need women like Wendy who will take those heartfelt desires seriously. God may be waiting to use you, through your prayer and discipline, in a very special way.

MY STUDY

Exodus 15:11; Psalm 66:5

The Intimate Heart

I pray... that all of them may be one, Father, just as you are in me and I am in you. May they also be in us so that the world may believe that you have sent me.

JOHN 17:20,21

Some years ago at a party, a famous actor was asked by a pastor to recite the Twenty-third Psalm. The actor agreed on the condition that the pastor recite it also.

The actor went first. With great poise, he began, "The Lord is my shepherd, I shall not want." The words flowed eloquently, like lovely music. When he finished, the audience applauded enthusiastically and gave him a standing ovation.

Now it was the pastor's turn. In his eighties, he'd lived his life walking closely with God. From the depths of his soul, he recited the familiar words. He knew every word, believed every word, and loved every word.

The audience fell silent; there was no applause, only tear-filled eyes. The actor said, "I have reached your eyes and your ears; this man of God has reached your hearts."

Intimacy has been defined as a close, sustained familiarity with another's inner life. Knowing God intimately makes the very essence of our lives radiate His love. Intimacy can be achieved only by mutual consent. God desires intimacy with you, but until you respond and seek Him with your whole heart, you will not experience true intimacy with Him.

Make it your heart's desire to know God intimately. His Word will give you insight into His character and personality, and His presence will give you a sense of peace that will give others a desire to know Him as well.

DAY 31

My good friend, Becky Tirabassi, is a fun-loving, vivacious lady who draws people like a magnet. On fire for the Lord, she's always praying for opportunities to touch someone with His love.

Becky told me about sitting down for her first appointment with Vicki, her manicurist. Becky explained that she was a Christian writer and speaker who came into that line of work because of her checkered past.

As an insecure teenager, Becky used alcohol and drugs to be accepted. By age nineteen, she was an alcoholic. At twenty-one, she attempted to break the addiction on her own. Withdrawal proved much more traumatic than she imagined possible. Consequently, her habits continued.

Finally, on the brink of suicide, Becky found her release. She met a kind man, a janitor, who explained that Jesus loved her unconditionally, even in her current state. In desperation, she agreed to pray with him, confessing her sins and accepting Christ's offer to make her a new creation.

Becky's life was dramatically and immediately transformed. Not only did God take away her desire to drink, but He also filled her with such joy and peace that she began telling everyone she knew what God had done.

Becky's transparency paved the way for further discussions with Vicki. Every week, their conversation revolved around spiritual matters.

Becky continued to pray for Vicki. It wasn't long before Vicki placed her faith in Jesus. She also asked Becky to help her conquer her addiction to alcohol.

Dear friend, you don't need a dramatic story like Becky's to share Christ effectively. But when you share, be sure to let people know how God has freed you from the bondage of sin. People relate to pain and failure. Don't be afraid to reveal the dark side of your past. It is there that God's light will shine ever so brightly!

HIS WORD

"Indeed, in our hearts we felt the sentence of death. But this happened that we might not rely on ourselves but on God, who raises the dead. He has delivered us from such a deadly peril, and he will deliver us" (2 Corinthians 1:9,10).

MY PART

What secrets from your past do you have? Are you reluctant to share these things? Ask God to help you be more open with those in need. Ask Him to give you peace and boldness to share with others how God has revealed Himself through these circumstances.

MY STUDY

1 Samuel 17:34–37; Psalm 4:1

Imagine trying to make an appointment with the President of the United States. He's quite busy!

Intercession

Yet think about this. Any believer can bow his or her head right now and speak directly with the Creator of the Universe. In fact, we have the awesome privilege of coming boldly to the throne of God at any time. This is a privilege not to be taken for granted!

God has given us the privilege of *intercessory* prayer, a special form of prayer that allows us to "stand in the gap" for others, to ask God to act on their behalf. Paul admonished Timothy about this: "I urge, then, first of all, that requests, prayers, intercession and thanksgiving be made for everyone—for kings and all those in authority" (1 Timothy 2:1,2).

Why is this so important? Paul went on to say, "...that we may live peaceful and quiet lives in all godliness and holiness. This is good, and pleases God our Savior" (vv. 2,3). According to this instruction, prayer for world leaders is a primary responsibility of the praying Christian.

Men and women in public office carry great responsibility and exert far-reaching influence. Their decisions affect the church, the city, the nation, and sometimes the world.

In modern times, we see God's actions change the course of history. For example, the beginning of *glasnost*, which preceded the fall of communism in the Soviet Union, began in February 1987—just one month after worldwide prayer for religious freedom for that country.

With God all things are possible. There is no need, no problem, no difficulty too great for God. He wants us to trust and believe Him so that we might plead with Him on behalf of others.

Let me urge you today, my friend, to call upon God's power. This is the time for all women to pray big prayers! Make intercession a regular part of your daily time with the Lord.

HIS WORD
"If my people, who are called by my name, will humble themselves and pray and seek my face and turn from their wicked ways, then will I hear from heaven and will forgive their sin and will heal their land" (2 Chronicles 7:14).

MY PART
"Oh, God, you have promised to heal us when we humble ourselves in prayer. We want to turn from our wicked ways and pray that you will help us to continue to seek Your face so that our prayers and our lives can make a difference. In Jesus' name, amen."

MY STUDY
Psalm 141:1,2; Ephesians 6:18

DAY 33

Chuck Swindoll tells a story set in England during World War II. Enemy bombing raids had destroyed much of historic London. Hundreds of men, women, and children were forced into the streets.

Reflections

Early one morning, while wandering through the rubble, an Allied soldier happened upon a young boy who had obviously been living off the meager scraps he could find. Longingly, the little guy had his nose pressed up against the window of a bakery.

Realizing the situation, the soldier slipped into the bakery to buy a few items. He went back outside and handed the boy a bag full of food.

The boy hesitated for a moment, then replied, "I don't have any money to pay for these."

The soldier lovingly answered, "I know. This is a gift."

The little boy looked at the bag, thought for a minute, and said, "Mister, are you God?"

Jesus said in John 14:9, "Anyone who has seen me has seen the Father." The life of Jesus reflected His Father's so closely that His behavior unmistakably represented God. All the qualities that are true of God are true of Jesus.

That's our mission, dear friend: to be a reflection of Jesus in the same way He's a reflection of the Father. Then, no matter what happens, others will see that there's Someone who loves them dearly and is there to meet them in their time of need.

That's a pretty tall order, and one that's absolutely impossible unless you've learned to trust Christ to live His life in and through you moment by moment. Through the power and control of the Holy Spirit, you can grow in your daily walk with Jesus Christ. You can become more like Him every day. Your life can reflect His beauty.

You might even catch yourself buying donuts for a small boy.

HIS WORD
"The Son of Man did not come to be served, but to serve, and to give his life as a ransom for many" (Matthew 20:28).

MY PART
With God's help, determine to maintain a moment by moment relationship with the Holy Spirit to help you reflect Jesus to others. Once His Holy Spirit empowers you, people will say they know what God is like— because they've seen something of Him in you!

MY STUDY
Proverbs 19:17; Isaiah 52:7

DAY 34

Miriam and Ney were inseparable, childhood friends. But over the years, they lost touch.

Old Friends

Recently, Ney was making plans to go to her high school reunion. She called to make plans with her dear friend. Miriam's husband answered and told her something shocking: "Ney, Miriam is dead." A year earlier Miriam had committed suicide.

My heart goes out to Miriam's husband and family —and to Ney. It's so easy to assume all is well in the life of another. No one ever knew how difficult life was for Miriam. Her lifelong friend, Ney, would love to have known. She would have immediately gone to Miriam in her time of need.

Hearing this was very sobering and poignant for me. It made me want to be in touch with old friends I've known and loved. Someone from long ago may need to know that I still care.

Does someone come to your mind? Has the Lord put someone on your heart that might appreciate a visit or a phone call from you today?

Perhaps you more closely identify with Miriam. Your

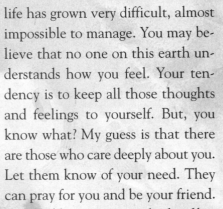

life has grown very difficult, almost impossible to manage. You may believe that no one on this earth understands how you feel. Your tendency is to keep all those thoughts and feelings to yourself. But, you know what? My guess is that there are those who care deeply about you. Let them know of your need. They can pray for you and be your friend.

God has put us in a body of believers to care for each other, pray for each other, and encourage one another. As the Bible says, "Let us consider how we may spur one another on toward love and good deeds ... Let us encourage one another— and all the more as you see the Day approaching" (Hebrews 10:24,25).

No, you can't help *everyone*, but don't let that stop you from helping *someone*.

HIS WORD
"When they were ill, I put on sackcloth and humbled myself with fasting. When my prayers returned to me unanswered, I went about mourning as though for my friend or brother. I bowed my head in grief as though weeping for my mother" (Psalm 35:13,14).

MY PART
Who needs to know you care deeply for her today? In the last few minutes, who has the Lord brought to your mind? Don't wait to be God's messenger. Pick up the phone. Give her a call today. You may be God's tool to reach the Miriam in your life.

MY STUDY
2 Samuel 9:1–7; Matthew 27:57–61

I once heard this story from Elizabeth Elliott.

It was Brenda's first rock-climbing trip. She was geared up and secured by a rope, ready for the climb.

The Unexpected

She started up the rock with lots of enthusiasm, headed for the peak. Out of breath, she stopped and looked above. There, before her, was a very difficult ledge.

When Brenda tugged on the rope, it swung around taut and hit her in the eye. And her contact lens popped out!

Precariously, she hung there, searching for the tiny lens on the granite rock. It was nowhere to be found, so she kept climbing.

An hour later, sitting at the peak, Brenda reflected on her climb. Her vision was impaired—great on one side, fuzzy on the other.

She thought about the verse that says, "The eyes of the Lord range throughout the earth" (2 Chronicles 16:9). She was convinced God knew exactly where her contact lens had fallen. Still, she was resigned to never finding the contact again.

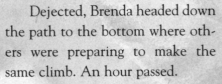

Dejected, Brenda headed down the path to the bottom where others were preparing to make the same climb. An hour passed.

Another girl, who had no idea of the missing contact, began to climb where Brenda had begun. Suddenly the girl let out an excited cry, "Hey, you guys! Did anyone lose a contact? There's an ant carrying a contact down the mountain!"

It was Brenda's contact!

Can you imagine that? God used a tiny ant to answer Brenda's prayer! There's nothing too small for Him to know. There's nothing too big for Him to handle. He will answer our prayers in ways we never imagined possible.

My friend, rest assured that God knows exactly where you dropped your lens. And it may be His sovereign plan to deliver it as you never expected! Special delivery. With love. From God.

HIS WORD
"When you did awesome things that we did not expect, you came down, and the mountains trembled before you" (Isaiah 64:3).

MY PART
Do you need an answer to prayer today? Need a raven to visit you, like the one that came to Elijah? How about an ant, like the one that delivered Brenda's contact? God will provide an answer, but it may not come as you expected. Are you struggling with a problem today? Pray. Then, expect the unexpected!

MY STUDY
Psalm 5:3; Mark 11:24

No matter how long we have been Christians, we all need to know important elements of prayer. The Creator of the Universe has openly invited His children to approach Him with our concerns. Here are five elements of prayer that can refresh your prayer life, help you teach others to pray, or bring new life to a group prayer meeting. Try it!

His Best

First, thank God for something—anything. Thank Him for His love, for a beautiful cloudless sky, for health, for a sound mind. Expressing gratitude to God can transform your attitude.

Second, thank God for something *specific* that's happened in the last day. Perhaps, it's gratitude for a quiet evening at home with a friend or loved one or safety for your children.

The third step is to pray a "Please help me" prayer. Ask God for help for yourself or someone else.

Fourth, ask God for something specific. I'm convinced that many times we have not because we ask not. Jesus is still asking, "What would you like me to do for you?" He's waiting for our petition.

Finally, thank God for how He will *answer* your prayers. When Jesus prayed in the garden right before His crucifixion, He asked God to take away His suffering. But Jesus knew that God is good, that God is always in control, and that it would be better to suffer than to disobey God.

Jesus concluded His prayer by saying, "I want Your will, not Mine." That's what you're doing when you expectantly thank God for how He'll answer your prayer.

Remember, your heavenly Father doesn't promise to give indiscriminately whatever we ask. Just like any father, He'll give only what is best for us.

So, let me urge you to go to your heavenly Father in prayer. He wants to hear from you, and He wants to give you His best.

Now, who can pass up that invitation? Get ready—you'll be amazed at what God can do!

HIS WORD

"Everyone who asks receives; he who seeks finds; and to him who knocks, the door will be opened" (Luke 11:10).

MY PART

"Lord Jesus, thank You for Your love and faithfulness. Thank You for the privilege of being able to come to You with my concerns. Thank You that You answer my prayers with every thought to my welfare. In Your holy name, amen."

MY STUDY

1 Kings 8:37–40; Psalm 66:16–20

When reading portions of the Old Testament, one man seems to stand out more than anyone else. His story is told with greater detail, his poetry is divinely inspired, and his example is continually held up for others to follow. That man's name is David.

David's Secret

What was David's secret? We know he wasn't perfect. He committed adultery; he compounded that sin by murder; and he suffered bouts of despair.

David's secret was his commitment and devotion to God—not just to the laws of God, though he valued them highly, but to God Himself. David and God had a dynamic, incredibly intimate relationship.

David sought the Lord every time he made a decision. He kept a tight rein on his emotions. And when he found something impure and displeasing to God, he repented. He loved the laws of God. When he broke those laws, his repentance was absolute.

Listen to David's total honesty and trust in God as he confessed his sin and made things right between himself and God:

Surely you desire truth in the inner parts; you teach me

wisdom in the inmost place... Hide your face from my sins and blot out all my iniquity. Create in me a pure heart, O God, and renew a steadfast spirit within me. Do not cast me from your presence or take your Holy Spirit from me. Restore to me the joy of your salvation and grant me a willing spirit, to sustain me... O Lord, open my lips, and my mouth will declare your praise (Psalm 51:6,9–12,15).

To David, even failure and horrible sin were opportunities to learn more about God. Through his weakness, David learned how dependent he was on God for having a pure heart and doing what is right. David loved the Lord wholeheartedly. His life was yielded to God with no reservations.

Dear friend, cultivate your relationship with God. Depend on Him and love Him wholeheartedly.

HIS WORD

"Jesus replied: 'Love the Lord your God with all your heart and with all your soul and with all your mind'" (Matthew 22:37).

MY PART

Read through all of Psalm 51. What emotions do you think David was feeling when he wrote these words? Is there any evidence of how God responded to David? How can you apply these thoughts to your life?

MY STUDY

Psalm 40:7,8; Jeremiah 3:13

DAY 38

Belinda clenched her teeth, holding back the impatience threatening to spill out. Her two-year-old Hilary was whimpering and pulling on her leg, demanding attention.

Refreshment

The toddler's wailing had started before the sun came up. Belinda hadn't enjoyed a moment to herself since then.

First, Hilary needed a diaper change. Then she needed to be fed. Then played with. Then comforted. Then changed again. Now Hilary wanted to play again.

"Lord," Belinda silently prayed, "I need some time with You. I don't have the strength to mother this precious child. How can I nurture her if I can't find the time to be nurtured by You?"

Even as Belinda cried in desperation, Hilary quit tugging at her leg. She toddled off to her room and began to play contentedly.

Bursting with gratitude, Belinda rushed to her own room and found her neglected Bible. She curled up in a chair to drink in the Word of God. Pouring out her heart to God and receiving His comfort, her soul was strengthened, her energy renewed.

Half an hour later, bright-eyed Hilary wandered into Belinda's room, announcing, "Mommy, I'm hungry!" This time Belinda responded to her child with love.

Isaiah 40:31 tells us exactly what to do when we're exhausted: "Those who wait for the LORD will gain new strength; they will mount up with wings like eagles, they will run and not get tired, they will walk and not become weary" (NASB). Waiting on the Lord requires listening to God and spending time reading His Word.

Belinda found that the only way she could be patient and loving with Hilary was to spend time with God.

But this principle is true in any circumstance. To endure the demands of life, it's essential to pray, read God's Word, and listen to His voice. My friend, let me encourage you to take time for this every day.

HIS WORD

"Repent, then, and turn to God, so that your sins may be wiped out, that times of refreshing may come from the Lord" (Acts 3:19).

MY PART

What has you feeling desperate today? Whether you're a single woman with lots of responsibility, a mother whose children have all left the nest, or a mother of young children like Belinda, you can find hope and rest by spending time with God frequently.

MY STUDY

Exodus 33:14; Psalm 142:1–3

When George Mathieson was a young man, he met and fell in love with a beautiful girl. They planned to be married after college graduation.

But George had a serious health condition that caused progressive blindness. As his blindness grew worse, his fiancée became scared. She couldn't imagine being married to a blind man, so she left him.

Can you imagine the devastation he felt? Losing his eyesight and the one he loved at the same time.

Twenty years later, he was *still* feeling a sense of loss. It surfaced while attending his sister's wedding. He made a willful decision to enter into the joy of her big day while his own heart was aching.

That night he went home and wrote a song that has become one of the greatest hymns of the church. The hymn is called, "O Love That Will Not Let Me Go." Maybe you're familiar with the words:

> O love that will not let me go,
> I rest my weary soul in Thee,
> I give Thee back the life I owe,
> That in its ocean depth
> Its flow may richer, fuller, be.

George Mathieson learned his *greatest lesson* at the point of his *greatest pain.*

Friend, when things are the worst, that's when God's love and His presence are the most real and meaningful. So often we're surprised when these hard times come our way, but we shouldn't be. We've had good warning. Jesus said, "In this world you will have trouble." But then He added, "But take heart! I have overcome the world" (John 16:33).

I wonder, has there been a time when you've been disappointed, even devastated by what's happened to you? Remember, God's love is as deep as the ocean. And He wants to meet you at your point of need, to let you know you're not alone. He loves you like no other can.

HIS WORD
"Everyone born of God overcomes the world. This is the victory that has overcome the world, even our faith" (1 John 5:4).

MY PART
"Loving heavenly Father, through the darkest of days I know You are always there to hold my hand, to guide me, and to comfort me. Thank You for Your never-ending love and care for me. I love You. Amen."

MY STUDY
1 Kings 8:56,57; Psalm 21:5–7

DAY 40

Brenda was hurrying through the supermarket when she knocked over a display of shoelaces. Embarrassed, she threw one packet into her cart and paid for it.

Shoelaces

She had stopped at the store to pick up a few things on her way to visit her friend, Donald, in the hospital. His arms and legs were paralyzed after he fell off a ladder.

"Brenda," Donald said when she arrived, "Sometimes I feel as though God just doesn't seem to care anymore."

All Brenda could say was, "You *know* He cares." As Brenda began to leave, Donald asked, "By the way, the nurse broke one of my shoestrings. Could you get me a new pair?"

Brenda opened her purse and pulled out the laces she had just bought and laced them into Donald's shoes.

They couldn't believe it! Even though Donald couldn't walk or tie his shoes, God had provided new laces just for him. Donald realized that if God cared about something as simple as his shoelaces, he certainly cared about his condition. The Lord does care about the details of life!

Jesus was in the boat with His disciples when a furious storm came up. Waves started breaking over the boat. The disciples looked for Jesus and found Him sleeping. Waking him, the disciples cried out, "'Lord, save us! We're going to drown!' He replied, 'You of little faith, why are you so afraid?' Then he got up and rebuked the winds and the waves, and it was completely calm" (Matthew 8:25,26).

Friend, God cared for Donald and for the disciples. But, just as important, He cares for *you*. He sees your needs, emotional or physical, down to the most minute detail.

So what's on *your* mind today? Are you riding the stormy sea? Or do you simply need a pair of shoelaces? God wants to provide for you. Open the door and, by faith, let Him in.

HIS WORD

"He is the Rock, his works are perfect, and all his ways are just. A faithful God who does no wrong, upright and just is he" (Deuteronomy 32:4).

MY PART

Make a serious study of the Scriptures relating to God's provision (such as Matthew 8 and 10). Then, as a practical reminder, over the next several days and weeks, whenever you tie your shoes, remember that God loves you and that He cares for every detail of your life.

MY STUDY

Psalm 98:2,3; Matthew 21:21,22

DAY 41

ary Ann was born with a cleft palate. As a student in Mrs. Leonard's second grade class, she felt very embarrassed when the other children asked her what happened to her lip.

One day Mrs. Leonard announced to the children that they'd be doing a whisper test to ensure that they had good hearing. She asked them to put one of their ears against the wall while she whispered into the other ear.

Usually Mrs. Leonard whispered something like "Your shoes are red," or "The sky is blue." But when it was Mary Ann's turn, Mrs. Leonard whispered seven unforgettable words.

She said in a hush, "I wish you were my little girl."

Oh, what a wonderful moment!

Sometimes we think our deficiencies make us unlovable. If anyone knew how bad we were, how ugly, how horrible, surely no one would claim us as their own, certainly not the Living God.

That must have been how the woman at the well felt in the Book of John, chapter four. She had at least three strikes against her the day she came to get water. She was a Samaritan, a cultural outcast according to Jewish tradition. She was a woman, an inferior member of her society. And she had a reputation for immorality. She had *every reason* to feel unworthy.

When Jesus began to speak with her, she was shocked. Why would this Jewish man talk to *her?* And with such *kindness!*

God loved this woman dearly. It frankly didn't matter what was wrong with her. He wanted to break through all the barriers that kept her from knowing Him. In essence, He whispered in her ear, "I wish you were my little girl."

And that is what He says to you right now. He loves you dearly!

He wants *you* to be His little girl. It's that simple. That, dear friend, is why they call it the Good News.

HIS WORD

"The LORD appeared to us in the past, saying: 'I have loved you with an everlasting love; I have drawn you with lovingkindness'" (Jeremiah 31:3).

MY PART

What challenges are you facing right now, today, this week? Your heavenly Father wants to hear your expression of what you are going through. Talk to Him and share the burdens of your heart. Give those burdens to Him. Then let Him carry those burdens and love you as only He can.

MY STUDY

Psalm 138:2;
Romans 8:38,39

In April 1994, Sharon was rushing to a choral rehearsal. Amazingly, the quarter-mile walk to her car left her huffing and puffing like never before.

The next day the doctor withdrew two liters of amber-colored fluid from her lungs. By the end of the week, Sharon's worst fears were confirmed. Cancer.

The first chemotherapy treatment was devastating. For eight days, she lay in her hospital bed suspended between life and death. All she could think was, *God, I know You love me, and I know You're here*. While she was surprised by her condition, she knew God was not.

Sharon said candidly, "I decided at some point in my life that if God were with me, the valley wouldn't be so terrible. Well, He was with me and He is with me, but it was still the valley. At times I could only get by minute-by-minute. I say this not to be dramatic, but to be honest."

Sharon went through five chemo treatments, lost all of her hair, had a bone marrow transplant, and a complete hysterectomy.

Then her doctor discovered that Sharon had micro-

scopic cancer. This disease can't be cured apart from a miracle.

Through all this, Sharon remained optimistic about the future. "Part of trusting God," she says, "is receiving each day as a gift and living it to the fullest." It means guarding your heart from despair or self-pity, retaining a good sense of humor, staying active and engaged in life.

Whether you're in a difficult situation right now or simply dealing with everyday life, remember, God meets you at the top of the mountain, and, surely, He meets you in the lowest valley.

To the end, Sharon lived each day to the fullest. She knew the character of God and understood that He loved her.

My friend, remember that life is a gift. Thank God for every day. Live life fully.

HIS WORD

"See how I love your precepts; preserve my life, O LORD, according to your love" (Psalm 119:159).

MY PART

"Lord Jesus, thank You for the privilege of life. I am but a breath, but You have seen fit to give me many days of life. Help me to live each day to the fullest through Your Spirit and for Your glory. In Your matchless name, amen."

MY STUDY

Nehemiah 9:5–7; 1 Timothy 6:11,12

DAY 43

When Corinne moved to Bulgaria with her husband and four children, she expected the adjustment to be stressful. But she had no idea how bad it would become.

Together

When they first arrived, they lived on the fifteenth floor of a dilapidated hotel with no elevator and no hot water. She was concerned about the safety of her children.

With almost no training in the language, Corinne was drained doing even basic activities. Corinne knew it would take at least two years to learn enough Bulgarian to share Christ with her first friend.

Initially, the stress caused Corinne to turn to the Lord for wisdom and strength. It was an adventure for the family, drawing them together.

Corinne admits she gradually began responding to the stress by withdrawing. Instead of trusting God, she tried to deal with everything alone. Instead of supporting her husband, Brooke, she tried to function independently.

She finally came to recognize her selfishness as sin. After discussion, Corinne and Brooke made an agreement. Whenever they felt the stress level rising, they would ask each other, "What is the one burden I can help you with?" With that question, they'd be willing to offer practical help.

We all know you don't have to go to Bulgaria to experience stress. No matter where you are, the principles Corinne learned are true for you, too.

Stress can be *good* when it produces growth in your relationship with God and your loved ones. Stress can be *bad* when it results in self-reliance and isolation from God and others. What makes the difference? Your attitude. You can either choose to trust God or to ignore Him and fend for yourself.

Let me urge you, friend, to aggressively make your relationships a priority during times of strain and struggle. Choosing to foster intimacy with God and your loved ones is the only way to survive the inevitable stress of life.

HIS WORD

"Rise up; this matter is in your hands. We will support you, so take courage and do it" (Ezra 10:4).

MY PART

Are you having difficulty connecting with your loved ones? Build into your schedule time to communicate concerns. If possible, take walks together. My husband and I have found nothing more productive than quiet time to share and pray together. These actions will strengthen any relationship.

MY STUDY

Psalm 2:11; Ephesians 2:22

DAY 44

Diana was just five years old when her mother died. Her father, overwhelmed with the responsibility of rearing six children, disappeared after the funeral. Diana and her five siblings were divided among relatives.

Free to Love

Placed with a loving aunt and uncle, Diana felt that she had finally found security.

But her happiness was short-lived. Within two years, her uncle died. Shortly thereafter, her aunt became ill. As Diana knelt beside her aunt's bed, she pleaded, "I'll do anything you want...just please don't die!" The thought of losing her precious aunt was unbearable.

The next morning, Diana learned that her aunt had died during the night. As she viewed the lifeless body, Diana told herself, *I'll never love anyone again. When I love someone, they die. I don't want people dying and leaving me anymore.* With that, Diana began to build an impenetrable fortress around her heart.

The years passed and Diana grew up. She eventually married a successful dentist and by age thirty-one, had four beautiful children. From the outside, Diana's life looked perfect. Inside, though, she was frightened—waiting for death to leave her abandoned once more.

One day, a friend invited Diana to a neighborhood Bible study. Much to her surprise, Diana found herself listening to the leader's every word. For the first time, she understood the message of God's love, that God gave His only Son to die for her so that she could know Him and have eternal life. Diana was impressed that Jesus promised to never leave her, to never abandon her. No one had been able to make that promise before!

In the security of God's love, the fortress around Diana's heart began to crumble. She asked Christ to come into her life. Diana felt truly free to love. The fear of being abandoned was gone and replaced with the love of a caring heavenly Father.

HIS WORD

"He who fears the LORD has a secure fortress, and for his children it will be a refuge" (Proverbs 14:26).

MY PART

You may have had experiences in your life where someone you love has abandoned you or turned his or her back on you. You're not alone. Thank God that He will always love you and will always be there for you.

MY STUDY

Deuteronomy 33:12; Hebrews 6:16–20

DAY 45

Loneliness often strikes when you least expect it—in a crowd or by yourself. Loneliness can stem from the death of a loved one, a romantic breakup, a serious illness, or a long-distance move.

His Comfort

God uses these feelings to stretch us, strengthen us, refine us, and help us to relate to a world that doesn't know Him.

Bonnie's most profound experience of loneliness began with a phone call from her doctor who explained that she would never conceive a child. Over the next few years, she and her husband, Rick, felt a deep sense of loss and grief, and Bonnie experienced intense loneliness.

Certain activities were painful. Bonnie specifically remembers the time she saw a group of children and their parents en route to a parade. As she looked at the sweet faces of the youngsters, the same intense longing swept over her.

She went home sobbing before the Lord. She poured out her pain, yelled out her frustration, pleaded for mercy. Then Bonnie experienced His presence in a new way. She knew God cared.

As Bonnie stopped trying to fill the emptiness with meaningless activity, she and Rick researched adoption agencies and submitted themselves to God's will. Ultimately, they both felt adoption was the right choice. An attitude of submission helped Bonnie move from self-pity to peaceful acceptance.

Many biblical heroes went through times when they were all alone but experienced God's power and faithfulness—people like Joseph, Moses, Jonah, Jeremiah, and Paul. Our Savior Jesus experienced loneliness in a way no one else has. Jesus even cried out, "My God, my God, why have you forsaken me?"

As Christians, we know nothing separates us from the love of God, and that suffering won't last forever.

God deeply loves and cares for you. I encourage you to accept loneliness from God as a gift—a time of pursuing depth in your relationship with Him.

HIS WORD

"Therefore, my dear friends, as you have always obeyed—not only in my presence, but now much more in my absence—continue to work out your salvation with fear and trembling, for it is God who works in you to will and to act according to his good purpose" (Philippians 2:12,13).

MY PART

In what ways are you lonely right now? Will you, by faith, thank God for this gift, this time to draw closer to Him? Then, as feelings of loneliness come over you, run into His loving arms. It is there that comfort awaits you.

MY STUDY

Genesis 39:19–23; Psalm 73:23,26

DAY 46

Every day, Sharon held an informal discussion with her first-graders that she called "family talks." These few moments were often the high point of the day, a time for students to express their feelings and ask questions.

With You

One morning, Sharon asked the class, "What do you enjoy most about the first grade?"

Little hands shot up immediately. Sharon thought their answers might be "recess" or "lunch time." Looking over her students, curly-haired Jeremy caught her attention. He was fidgeting and wildly waving his hand. Sharon asked, "What do you like best, Jeremy?"

His answer burst forth, "I like being with you!"

Sharon loved that. That simple declaration reminded her that it's not recess or lunch time that means the most to a child. It's the relationship that has the deepest influence.

On the way home, she pondered what had happened. She thought about her relationship with God. Sharon valued all she was learning about God. But most of all, she was growing in her appreciation of just being in the Lord's presence—just being with Him.

What about you? What do you enjoy most about God? Can you answer with the enthusiasm of Jeremy that it's the relationship you enjoy the most, just being with Him?

There's no formula to enjoying a deeper, more intimate relationship with God. Just like any relationship, it takes time. And that's where I find many women missing out. The demands of life become a huge distraction for one of the most enjoyable, fulfilling, and meaningful aspects of life in Christ.

Being a Christian isn't only what God does for us; it's the relationship *with Him* that gives meaning and purpose to our whole life.

Find time to be with God. As your relationship with Him grows, you'll discover how much pleasure and joy there is in knowing Him. His delight is in hearing us say, "I like being with you."

HIS WORD
"The man who loves God is known by God" (1 Corinthians 8:3).

MY PART
Set aside time each day to spend with God. Perhaps early in the morning, or late at night. Maybe you could make your coffee break a time to read one of the psalms or a portion of a devotional book. You may also find time alone while in the car. In those brief moments, spend time with God.

MY STUDY
Nehemiah 1:11; Psalm 119:174–176

DAY 47

As a young Christian in college, Shirley joyfully spent hours reading God's Word. But the joy Shirley experienced eventually began to fade. She reached her first spiritual slump as a busy wife and mother. Receiving little encouragement, she began to withdraw from other Christians.

Returning

Shirley felt as though she had nothing to give. She had ritual instead of joyful communion.

Gradually, she found herself drawn back to God's Word. She set open Bibles on the kitchen counter, on the dining room table, and in the bedroom. As she worked around the house, Shirley would read the verses and meditate on them.

As she let God's Word soak into her heart, her attitude began to change. Once again that delight in God was part of her life.

Many years later, entering a new season of life, Shirley found herself in another spiritual slump. She didn't feel like doing much of anything and wanted a break. Unfortunately, she also took a break from regularly meeting with God.

Instead, she read other books, watched television, or played computer games. She distracted herself and lost her delight in God.

Facing another spiritual rut, this time Shirley knew how to return to her first love for God. She committed to focusing her attention on His Word.

This meant turning off the television and the computer and picking up her Bible. It meant carving out some special time to take a walk, to pray, and to read. It meant joining a Bible study to be around other Christians who could encourage and pray for her.

Oh, dear friend, life in Christ is a process, an ongoing adventure that never ends. So if you feel as Shirley did, a bit discouraged at times, don't give up! Continue to pursue the One you love. Allow Him to renew your spirit and to refresh your heart.

HIS WORD

"Jesus answered, 'It is written: "Man does not live on bread alone, but on every word that comes from the mouth of God"'" (Matthew 4:4).

MY PART

Can you relate to Shirley's story? You may be saying to yourself, That's me. I feel like that! Well, friend, there's hope. Ask God to give you strength as you let go of the things distracting you from Him. Then be diligent, taking time to maintain a closeness with Him.

MY STUDY

Psalm 35:9; Jeremiah 15:16

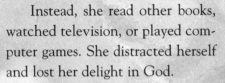

The ladies were taking their places around elegantly decorated tables, but Alice was standing alone in the middle of the room. There was no place for her to sit.

He Understands

For a moment, she stood frozen, her mind racing backward in time. She was transported back forty-five years, right into Mrs. Isabel's first-grade classroom. It was her first day at the school. She was the "new kid" once again.

Because there weren't enough desks in the classroom, Alice was seated at a table next to the wall, well away from the other children. In that remote place, she was often overlooked when supplies were passed out. She *felt* left out.

Back in the present, those old feelings caused tears to well in her eyes as she watched the hostesses quickly preparing another table for the overflow crowd. Throughout the luncheon, Alice maintained her composure. But when she got in her car to leave, the floodgates opened. She cried and told God about the pain.

She was convinced that He was trying to teach her something by stirring up those old feelings. God reminded Alice that His Son, Jesus, endured intense times of rejection.

His earthly life was filled with rejection. The night before His arrest, rather than join Him in His anguish, the disciples slept. At His trial, His closest companions abandoned Him. On the cross, Jesus suffered great emotional agony when He was separated from God the Father.

As Alice began to think on these things, she was comforted in knowing that God understands. She thought, *He's been right where I've been*. In this truth, she found peace and comfort.

My friend, I don't know what you're going through, but God does, and He understands. Isaiah 53:3 says Jesus was "despised and rejected by men, a man of sorrows, and familiar with suffering."

Whatever you are feeling today, rest assured, my friend. God truly understands.

HIS WORD

"I tell you the truth, you will weep and mourn while the world rejoices. You will grieve, but your grief will turn to joy" (John 16:20).

MY PART

"Lord, there are times when I feel rejected by others. I know that You understand how I feel. Thank You for Your comfort and peace during those times. Thank You for Your loving Spirit who draws me close to You. Amen."

MY STUDY

Psalm 10:14; Lamentations 3:31–33

DAY 49

As a city girl, Jeanne often went to visit cousins in the country. Her cousin Tom was just a year older, but he was much wiser in the ways of country living. And he loved scaring Jeanne.

Focus

There was a swinging bridge stretching high above a rushing stream. Made of flexible steel cables and wooden slats, the bridge swayed with every step.

Whenever Jeanne went to visit, Tom always had something to show her—on the other side of the bridge! He would run across the bridge first. On the other end, he'd stand waiting. Yelling at Jeanne to hurry up, he'd grab the cables and shake them as hard as he could.

Not as sure-footed, Jeanne held on for dear life. Frozen with fright, she'd beg him to stop. The more she pleaded for him to stop, the harder he laughed and taunted her.

Finally, Jeanne had had enough. She begged her dad to make Tom stop. But Jeanne's wise father told her she was the only one who could do that.

He told Jeanne that when she was on the bridge she mustn't look down or yell, and she must keep walking.

She should then focus her eyes on the great big tree trunk in front of her to which the bridge cable was attached and walk toward it.

It sounded like great advice. So when Tom wasn't around, Jeanne practiced. She learned to walk across that bridge with confidence!

That's a great illustration about walking with God. At times, it feels like someone's on the other side shaking the very cables of our lives. Sometimes we forget to Whom those cables are attached.

On those days—when the children are demanding, your husband isn't being very understanding, or your boss is really crabby—look up and keep your eyes on Jesus. Focus on Him and keep walking with confidence.

HIS WORD

"When Jesus spoke again to the people, he said, 'I am the light of the world. Whoever follows me will never walk in darkness, but will have the light of life'" (John 8:12).

MY PART

To focus on Jesus is to take Him into account in every situation. As you race through those difficult days, stop for just a minute and call out to Him. Be specific. Ask Him to give you His peace. Then keep walking in faith.

MY STUDY

*Psalm 23:4;
Isaiah 55:6*

Thirty years ago, a young girl was raped by someone she trusted. She naively drank until she passed out. Then her boyfriend raped her. She became pregnant.

Born Again

Horrified, she considered suicide. Her dad, a prominent politician, took her immediately to a city where he'd arranged an adoption. When she realized this, she protested. She wanted to keep the baby.

Her father then insisted she marry the baby's father. All trust and respect for this boy had been lost, but her father overruled, and they were married.

A baby boy was born, but the relationship was never restored. They were divorced.

This girl's life had been one disaster after another. She'd been brought up in church but kept God "on a shelf," to be used when she needed Him. She had no idea how He could help her now.

Her son, conceived in such unfortunate circumstances, grew up and entered Stanford University. While there, he became a Christian through the Campus Crusade for Christ ministry.

When he went home, he said to his mom, "I've been born again." She was stunned. "How could you be? I'm the one who gave you birth!" He tried to explain, but she didn't understand.

The night before her fortieth birthday, she decided to tell her son the circumstances of his birth. She also prayed that night to a God she'd never known. "Oh, God, I don't know how to be born again. But I promise you, I'll read this Bible every day of my life."

She kept that promise and came to know Jesus personally.

Dear friend, God can do anything. He's never limited by unfortunate circumstances or mistakes. God is never "on the shelf," and He has the most creative ways of resolving horrifying dilemmas. All we need is to trust Him. As Romans 8:28 says, "In all things God works for the good of those who love him."

HIS WORD
"'Do not let your hearts be troubled. Trust in God; trust also in me. In my Father's house are many rooms; if it were not so, I would have told you. I am going there to prepare a place for you'" (John 14:1,2).

MY PART
"All-powerful God, because You control heaven and earth, I can trust You with my life. Because You love me infinitely, I can trust You with my heart. Thank You for watching over me, guiding me, and protecting me. In Your Son's holy name, amen."

MY STUDY
Psalm 20:6–8; Jeremiah 39:17,18

Growing up in the Scottish countryside, Sheila Walsh was surrounded by sheep. She tells stories showing parallels between sheep and shepherds and her relationship with her Savior.

The Shepherd

Sometimes in a herd of sheep, a headstrong lamb will refuse to submit to its master. Such rebellion is very dangerous for the little lamb. If it wanders off, it could get into serious trouble.

In such cases, the shepherd takes the misbehaving lamb and breaks its leg. While it seems cruel and painful, the shepherd knows that, in the long run, it's the loving thing to do. The shepherd then puts the lamb on his shoulders and carries it around until the leg heals.

During that process, the shepherd and the wayward sheep form a bond that's never broken. When the lamb heals, the shepherd sets him "free," but the lamb stays close by, never striking out in rebellious independence again.

Sheila says as a younger person, she was independent, self-sufficient, wanting to go her own way. Then she came to a place of brokenness. She realized that controlling her own life left her in big trouble. She turned to her loving heavenly Father and surrendered to His will.

She saw God's love in a way that she'd never known and her intimacy with Him became the core of her life. She never wandered away again.

"Interestingly," she says, "in my time of need, God didn't show me my bright future to help me get through the despair. He showed me Himself. Then I knew that no matter what the future held, He would hold me and I had nothing to fear."

Oh, dear friend, God is completely trustworthy. His faithfulness knows no bounds, and His love never ends.

Don't be like the lamb that only learns the lesson when its leg is broken. Learn it from God's own Word, "The Lord is *your* shepherd." And He takes good care of His sheep.

HIS WORD

"'I am the good shepherd. The good shepherd lays down his life for the sheep'" (John 10:11).

MY PART

"Lord Jesus, You are the Great Shepherd. When I stray from Your care, You find me and return me to the fold. When I rebel from Your leadership, You lovingly do what's necessary to keep me out of harm's way. You always take good care of me. Thank You. Amen."

MY STUDY

Psalm 80:1,2; Ezekiel 34:11–13

DAY 52

Friends are a special gift from God. When Virelle's best friend moved two thousand miles away, Virelle felt utterly alone. She appreciated her friend's wit and godly advice. Her feeling of withdrawal from the daily conversations left her wondering if anyone would ever again understand her.

Best Friend

Then one morning, Virelle sensed God asking, "How about letting Me be your best friend?" Proverbs 18:24 says, "There is a friend who sticks closer than a brother." As she tried the idea, she discovered four truths about God's friendship that changed her life:

- God listens when no one else will. At any time of the day or night, you can call out to God and He will listen to your prayers.

- God knows you thoroughly and loves you anyway. God knew you before you were born. He knows your heart and every thought in your head—good and bad. But He still gave the life of His Son for you because He loves you.

- God acts powerfully on your behalf. He can do what

earthly friends cannot. God has sovereign control of the universe. He is capable of doing anything for you, and He is faithful to do only what is best for you.

- God craves closeness with you. As your heavenly Father, God longs to hear from you, to help you with your problems, and to comfort and bless you.

My friend, the next time you feel lonely or feel there is no one to talk to, remember that God is one friend who will never move away and is always there to help. As it says in Jeremiah 33:3, "Call to me and I will answer you and tell you great and unsearchable things you do not know." God not only wants to be your friend, He wants to have an intimate relationship with you. What more could you ask from a friend?

HIS WORD
"Now may the Lord of peace himself give you peace at all times and in every way. The Lord be with all of you" (2 Thessalonians 3:16).

MY PART
Talk to God as you would your closest friend. Tell Him what's on your mind and what's on your heart. You might even try using a notebook as a journal to record your conversations and prayers. Set aside daily time and make it a priority in your life.

MY STUDY
Psalm 142:1,2; Isaiah 44:23

Cheryl loves students, and she has developed a dynamic ministry among them. But after ten years, she was burned out—life became routine and passionless. "Life seemed to be crumbling in around me," she wrote. "I wanted to drop out."

Seek Him

One night she cried out in desperation, "Jesus, I know You're supposed to be enough, but You do not feel like enough. Please help me."

Cheryl was honest with God. And He answered her desperate prayer by filling her heart with His presence.

God wants us to seek Him no matter what we are feeling, even if we are having doubts about Him working in our lives. The Bible tells us in 1 Chronicles 16:10,11, "Glory in his holy name; let the hearts of those who seek the LORD rejoice. Look to the LORD and his strength; seek his face always." This verse tells us several things.

First, we are to glory in His name. His name holds the power of the universe, so it is worthy of honor and praise.

Next, we are to seek the Lord. Seeking God is a conscious, willful act on our parts.

Then, as we are seeking the Lord, we should rejoice because we know that He hears our prayers and is faithful to answer them. He is the source of our strength.

Finally, it says we are to "seek his face always." No matter what we are going through or how we are feeling—happy, sad, apathetic—we should seek after Him, to see Him up close and personal, face-to-face.

If that isn't encouraging enough, look at Proverbs 8:17, which says, "I love those who love me, and those who seek me find me." What a wonderful promise!

Friend, don't drop out. Instead, seek Him diligently and desperately. Get to know Him. Be honest with God. Talk with Him. He is always there to be your strength.

HIS WORD

"If from there you seek the LORD your God, you will find him if you look for him with all your heart and with all your soul" (Deuteronomy 4:29).

MY PART

"Lord Jesus, You are worthy of all praise, honor, and glory. I earnestly seek You as the source of my comfort and strength. My heart rejoices in thankfulness of Your love for me and Your openness to me. May I always seek Your face. Amen."

MY STUDY

Psalm 27:4; Colossians 3:1

Dr. Bruce Waltke is an Old Testament scholar. He recently stated, "We are never more like God than when we make unconditional vows of commitment to one another."

Covenant

Dr. Waltke was speaking of the marriage relationship, the most important covenant relationship humans can have with each other. A covenant is an agreement or bond. When we make commitments to each other in the context of marriage, we have God's covenant with us to use as our model.

Covenants are very important to God. When God makes an agreement, it is permanently binding. Psalm 105:8 tells us, "[God] remembers his covenant forever, the word he commanded, for a thousand generations." What wonderful security it is to know that when God makes a covenant, it will stand true for eternity. This covenant demonstrates unyielding commitment.

In the New Testament, God established a new covenant with His people. "In the same way, after the supper he took the cup, saying, 'This cup is the new covenant in my blood, which is poured out for you'"

(Luke 22:20). Christ gave His blood as a sacrifice for our sins.

Marriage is also a covenant that requires commitment and sacrifice. In the marriage relationship, it is assumed that both parties are committed to each other and are willing to sacrifice their own desires for the benefit of the union. In a biblical marriage, a man and a woman become one flesh—a unit joined by God to love each other, serve each other, and serve God.

Dear friend, don't let the modern attitudes of disposable marriages influence your own marriage. Honor the commitment before God that you made to your husband. Honor it in word, in thought, and in deed. This is contrary to what the world teaches. All around us we hear that we have a right to break up our marriage if we are not happy or fulfilled. But God will honor you for your faithfulness, and you will be blessed.

HIS WORD

"*I will maintain my love to him forever, and my covenant with him will never fail*" (Psalm 89:28).

MY PART

"*Faithful God and Savior, thank You for Your commitment and sacrifice. Help me to show love toward my spouse in the same way You have shown love toward me. Help me to have a marriage of commitment, sacrifice, and love. In Your holy name, amen.*"

MY STUDY

Genesis 9:11–13; Galatians 3:14–16

DAY 55

As a single woman, Nancy used the television for noise and companionship, but through it she was becoming desensitized to what was spiritually important.

The Mind

She said, "I knew my walk with God would be clearer, fresher, more fruitful and whole if I'd just turn off the TV. Finally, I raised the white flag of surrender." She promised God she wouldn't watch television whenever she was alone.

The Bible tells us in Romans 12:2, "Do not conform any longer to the pattern of this world, but be transformed by the renewing of your mind. Then you will be able to test and approve what God's will is—his good, pleasing and perfect will."

As followers of Christ, we are to be constantly in the process of renewing our minds to contrast with the pattern of this world. As we do this, we will be better able to discern God's will for our life.

Our minds are constantly being bombarded with information. If we are putting the wrong information into our minds, we will find ourselves less peaceful and less able to resist the temptations of the flesh. That is why God listed in a very specific way the kinds of things we should spend our time thinking about.

Philippians 4:8 gives us a helpful list of items with which we are to fill our minds. We are told, "Finally, brothers, whatever is true, whatever is noble, whatever is right, whatever is pure, whatever is lovely, whatever is admirable—if anything is excellent or praiseworthy —think about such things."

Be careful, my friend, what you expose your mind to. If we think about evil things, we will exhibit evil actions. If we think about righteous things, we are more likely to exhibit righteous, Christlike actions. Let the things of Christ so permeate your thoughts and your life that there is no room for anything else.

HIS WORD

"The mind of sinful man is death, but the mind controlled by the Spirit is life and peace" (Romans 8:6).

MY PART

Monitor the kind of information to which you expose your mind. Study Philippians 4:8. Take each of the eight subjects mentioned and write down a few thoughts or events in your life applicable to each subject. Throughout the day, think about these things.

MY STUDY

Psalm 119:37; Isaiah 26:3

Some people believe becoming a Christian will solve all the problems they face. Unfortunately, it isn't that simple.

His Light

Lisa learned this lesson in her own life. Her temptations for alcohol and promiscuity didn't immediately go away after she came to know Christ. Even though she was determined to please God with her new discipline and purity, overcoming the temptations was a real struggle.

One night, in desperate frustration, Lisa realized she needed to surrender every part of her life to the power of the Holy Spirit. Since that night more than three years ago, Lisa has not had another drink and has remained sexually pure.

I wonder, is there a habit that plagues you? Something difficult to let go?

In Luke 9:23 Jesus tells us, "If anyone would come after me, he must deny himself and take up his cross daily and follow me." Each day we must make the conscious choice to deny ourselves, including the desires of the flesh, take up our cross, and follow Christ. Living the Christian life is a day-by-day walk.

But we do not walk alone. Christ is there with us to light our way. Jesus said, "I am the light of the world. Whoever follows me will never walk in darkness, but will have the light of life" (John 8:12).

We also have the power of His Spirit to help us withstand temptation. Romans 8 tells us, "If by the Spirit you put to death the misdeeds of the body, you will live, because those who are led by the Spirit of God are sons of God" (vv. 13,14).

As you walk through the Christian life, let Christ in you light your way. Depend on the power of the Holy Spirit to give you strength. Soon, the temptations won't be as tempting anymore. You will experience victory.

HIS WORD
"He gives strength to the weary and increases the power of the weak" (Isaiah 40:29).

MY PART
"Lord Jesus, my Savior, You are the light in a dark world. You are the strength for a weak body. Thank You for living Your life in me to be my guide and my strength. Through your power, help me to stand against any temptations that come my way today or any day. In Your holy name, amen."

MY STUDY
Psalm 28:7;
Matthew 26:41

Kay Arthur is a well-known and much-loved author and Bible teacher. But it wasn't always so.

Kay's life came crashing down when she divorced the man of her dreams. That started her search for love.

His Power

She led an immoral lifestyle for several years. At the end of her rope, she turned to Jesus. Kay prayed to God to take control of her life and give her peace. Her life was immediately transformed. She began a personal quest through the Scriptures.

Eventually, Kay met and fell in love with a single missionary named Jack Arthur. They have enjoyed many wonderful years of marriage together.

Her life is such a testimony of what God can do with imperfect people.

There was another imperfect person. A man named Saul, who became the apostle Paul, was a Jewish persecutor of Christians. He was zealous for his cause. But one day on the road to Damascus, the Lord visited Saul. He blinded him for three days. Saul's companions led him into Damascus. There, God restored Saul's sight through a man named Ananias, and Saul was dramatically transformed.

In Acts 9 we read about what Saul did after he was healed: "Saul spent several days with the disciples in Damascus. At once he began to preach in the synagogues that Jesus is the Son of God. All those who heard him were astonished and asked, 'Isn't he the man who raised havoc in Jerusalem among those who call on this name? And hasn't he come here to take them as prisoners to the chief priests?' Yet Saul grew more and more powerful and baffled the Jews living in Damascus by proving that Jesus is the Christ" (vv. 19–22).

God is not discouraged by your flaws. God takes you as you are and, through the power of His Spirit, transforms you into the person He wants you to be. Let God transform your life, moment by moment.

HIS WORD

"Summon your power, O God; show us your strength, O God, as you have done before" (Psalm 68:28).

MY PART

What temptations do you face each day? As you face them, remind yourself that God has given you His Spirit as a resource, to give you strength against temptations. Each morning, ask God to keep you from temptation, then rely on His strength.

MY STUDY

Joshua 4:23,24; 2 Corinthians 13:4

DAY 58

My friend's friend is a gifted, caring, attractive woman in her early fifties. She's a devoted mother and grandmother who's been a Christian all her adult life.

His Counsel

More than ten years ago, this woman left her husband of fifteen years. They were active in church, and her husband was a deacon. But he was disappointing to her. He was faithful and had many friends, but he couldn't keep a job.

He bored easily and hopped from job to job seeking a better position. He was charming, but irresponsible. This woman could hardly bear his lack of motivation, and she became disgusted with her own spirit, which had become nagging and negative. Convinced it was better to be on her own than to continue in this stagnant, frustrating atmosphere, she divorced him.

In the years since, she's lived in several cities, and has gone from job to job just to make ends meet. She struggles to sustain herself financially. Her children are now adults, so she lives alone in a small apartment.

Her husband remarried and has remained his social,

jovial self.

My friend has asked this woman, "Do you ever regret your decision to leave your husband?" Sadly, she said, "Yes, I really do. And it's caused so much pain for my children and even my grandchildren. I had no idea it would be so hard on them. The scars are very deep."

I don't know all the circumstances of her life and marriage or the agony and fear she felt. I do know this. Sometimes, the easy way out, isn't.

Often, in our effort to rescue ourselves from a difficult place, we make poor choices. Sometimes we opt for a permanent solution to a temporary problem. Sometimes we think something is impossible when it isn't.

Dear friend, be very careful about the choices you make today. Seek God's counsel diligently. Let His Word and His Spirit guide you.

HIS WORD

"Since you are my rock and my fortress, for the sake of your name lead and guide me" (Psalm 31:3).

MY PART

Is there something in your life right now that you feel you can't bear for one more day? Perhaps you're on the verge of making a very big decision, one you'll have to live with for the rest of your life. Let God meet you where you are. Let Him be your solution.

MY STUDY

Isaiah 57:18; Luke 12:30–32

DAY 59

In the first century, a woman's value was determined primarily by the social status of her husband and by the number of male children she bore. But Mary, the sister of Martha and Lazarus, pushed those boundaries.

Jesus and His disciples had been traveling near Bethany. As they passed through the village, Martha invited the whole group to stay in her home. No sooner had Martha extended the invitation than her sister Mary became fascinated with their houseguest. The Bible says she "sat at the Lord's feet listening to what he said."

Mary's position seated at Jesus' feet was traditionally reserved for males only. No woman could be taught by a rabbi in this way. According to the first-century norms, both Jesus and Mary were violating very explicit social and religious customs observed by all devout Jews.

Then Martha complained that she was left to do the kitchen work all on her own. Let me suggest there was something more behind Martha's frustration. She knew Mary was out of place by sitting at Jesus' feet, and she was concerned about protecting the reputation of her family. If anyone heard about what Mary had done, they'd be the laughingstock of the town.

That's when Jesus responded, with kindness, "Martha, Martha, you are worried and upset about many things, but only one thing is needed. Mary has chosen what is better, and it will not be taken away from her" (Luke 10:41,42).

Jesus was willing to break the social mores in order to have Mary at His feet. He honored her desire to learn from Him.

My dear friend, don't let *anyone* sell you the lie that Christianity suppresses or devalues women. Let's take our cues from Jesus. He invites all of us, men and women, to sit at His feet, to listen and to learn from Him.

HIS WORD

"A voice came from the cloud, saying, 'This is my Son, whom I have chosen; listen to him'" (Luke 9:35).

MY PART

In your time with God today, try something a little different. Take your Bible and a pillow or blanket and sit on the floor. As you read God's Word, think of yourself sitting at Jesus' feet, listening to the words coming out of His mouth. Respond in prayer to what you have read.

MY STUDY

Psalm 73:28; Lamentations 3:56–58

DAY 60

Brielle and Kyrie Jackson are twin sisters. Born twelve weeks premature, their entrance into the world was dramatic. *Reader's Digest* told their tender story.

Better Than One

Kyrie was the big sister at two pounds, three ounces. She gained weight and slept calmly. Brielle, however, had a more difficult start. She had breathing and heart-rate problems. The oxygen level of her blood was low. She lagged *far* behind.

At about a month old, Brielle's condition suddenly worsened. She gasped for breath, turned bluish, and her heart rate increased rapidly.

The parents watched closely and were terribly afraid they'd lose her. The nurses tried everything medically possible. Still, Brielle showed no sign of improvement.

One of the nurses then asked the parents for permission to try a procedure she'd read about that was common practice in Europe. With their permission, the nurse put the babies in the same incubator! It wasn't a fancy medical procedure, but it wasn't the norm, either.

In an instant, the sick baby snuggled up to her sister. She calmed and her vital signs improved signifi-

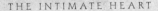

cantly. As she dozed, Kyrie wrapped her small arm around her tiny sister.

Soon little Brielle was gaining strength. Eventually, both girls became strong and healthy. What a miracle!

The Book of Ecclesiastes says, "Two are better than one, because they have a good return for their work: if one falls down, his friend can help him up" (4:9,10).

That's so true. God's design is for each person to be in relationship with others. Working together. Helping one another. It's true in daily life, in the work of ministry, and in prayer.

When you feel weak and inadequate, nothing helps like having a friend. One who is stronger, at least at the moment! There's great encouragement in someone hearing your heart and helping you carry a burden.

Two *are* better than one, my friend.

HIS WORD

"*May the God who gives endurance and encouragement give you a spirit of unity among yourselves as you follow Christ Jesus, so that with one heart and mouth you may glorify the God and Father of our Lord Jesus Christ*" (Romans 15:5,6).

MY PART

"*Father God, Thank You for the people that You have placed around me. Thank You for the times when I can support them and for the times when they can support me. Thank You most of all that You are the greatest friend of all. Amen.*"

MY STUDY

Psalm 133:1; Isaiah 41:13

The Growing Heart

Perseverance must finish its work so
that you may be mature and complete,
not lacking anything.

JAMES 1:4

In our culture, achievement and success are applauded and rewarded. We use the power of affirmation even with those of a very young age. With cheers of joy and claps of applause, parents coax their baby to take those first brave steps. As the toddler wobbles into open arms, their smiles affirm the great accomplishment. Their encouragement helps the baby keep trying until he can successfully walk without assistance.

In our walk with Christ, we are not called to be successful, but we are called to be faithful. Even if our spiritual steps are unsteady at times, we must press on. Developing a life of faithfulness requires our careful attention to choices we make every day. In most cases, the seemingly insignificant little things may be pivotal to our desire to be faithful to God.

Every event in our lives presents an opportunity for us to grow. God wants us to mature and develop a faith that will sustain us through the difficult times in our lives. He rewards us when we persevere. God's faithfulness gives us the assurance and encouragement that we can grow in our expression of faithfulness to Him.

Every time you take a negative thought captive or share your faith with a friend, you are taking "baby steps" of faith and your heavenly Father is pleased with your growth. Each new step is an achievement. And heaven cheers!

Pride is an insidious enemy, creeping unsuspected into our hearts and minds. Left unattended, it will destroy us. Humility, on the other hand, is the source of life.

Poor in Spirit

From our earliest days we are nurtured by secular philosophy, which says we've got to believe in ourselves, express ourselves, and have self-confidence; we must be independent, self-assured, and self-reliant. Our culture says these qualities make us successful. But without God, my friend, all of these are pride. Pure and simple.

Through the Beatitudes, given by Jesus, we see a compelling scale by which our pride should be measured. Jesus said, "Blessed are the poor in spirit, for theirs is the kingdom of heaven" (Matthew 5:3). What does this mean?

Being poor in spirit doesn't mean suppressing a vivacious personality. Nor does it mean becoming a doormat. Instead, it defines how we view ourselves and how we come face to face with God. To be poor in spirit is to realize our need for a Savior.

Let me share the insightful words of Max Lucado from his wonderful book, *The Applause of Heaven:*

You don't impress the officials at NASA with a paper airplane. You don't boast about your crayon sketches in the presence of Picasso. You don't claim equality with Einstein because you can write $E=MC^2$. And you don't boast about your goodness in the presence of the Perfect.

The jewel of joy is given to the impoverished spirits, not the affluent. God's delight is received upon surrender, not awarded upon conquest. The first step to joy is a plea for help, an acknowledgment of moral destitution. Those who taste God's presence have declared spiritual bankruptcy and are aware of their spiritual crisis. They don't brag. They beg.

Don't be deceived. God does not value selfish pride. Only when we realize our own inadequacy are we then able to experience the fullness of God's power and blessing in our lives.

HIS WORD
"Woe to those who are wise in their own eyes and clever in their own sight" (Isaiah 5:21).

MY PART
Have you been deceived? Are you placing too much trust in your own ability to perform? Ponder your own helplessness to redeem your life and trust in Christ's righteousness to save and forgive. Have confidence, not in yourself, but in the God who loves you and gives you life.

MY STUDY
Proverbs 22:4; Matthew 5:3–10

DAY 62

The Christian life is not difficult. No, it's not difficult at all. It's impossible!

Have you really come to grips with that truth? Or do you continue to strive for perfection?

Almost every day I talk to Christian women who constantly feel frustrated and defeated in their lives. They say things like, "I try to do what I'm supposed to do, but I just can't."

Barbara is a dear friend who came to know Christ when she was about thirty. She went to church, taught Sunday school, and by all outward appearances, seemed like a model Christian woman. Yet inside, she was miserable.

She talked about *love*...but deep down, she held hatred in her heart.

She talked about the *peace* of God...but Barbara was prone to worry herself silly.

She spoke of *patience*...but her family knew about her short fuse.

No matter how hard Barbara tried, nothing seemed to work.

Then one day, a friend told her how she could walk in the power and control of the Holy Spirit and explained that the Christian life was not difficult—it was impossible. Only through a complete surrendering to the Holy Spirit could Barbara ever be all she was created to be. Barbara realized the freedom of placing her life in God's hands and living by His power.

No one can live the perfect Christian life except Jesus Christ. He lived an absolutely sinless life. But what's amazing is that He wants to give us the power to live that kind of life, too. We can't achieve sinless perfection on this earth, but He wants to live His life in and through us right now.

Dear friend, like Barbara, you can depend on God moment by moment. He will give you the strength to make right choices and maintain proper attitudes.

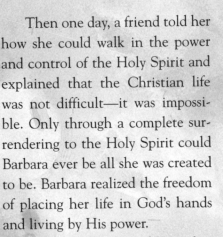

HIS WORD
"If the Spirit of him who raised Jesus from the dead is living in you, he who raised Christ from the dead will also give life to your mortal bodies through his Spirit, who lives in you" (Romans 8:11).

MY PART
Jesus promised, "I will give you a Helper to be with you and to abide in you." That Helper is the Holy Spirit, and He empowers us to follow Christ as we should. This life-changing power is the key to supernatural living. Ask God to transform your efforts into trusting in Him to meet your need.

MY STUDY
Psalm 31:5; Ezekiel 36:27

DAY 63

Today's woman is a busy woman. Her world is filled with responsibility and distractions. Whether single, married, working, or staying at home, her daily schedule includes a continual series of tasks, punctuated by little surprise detours along the way.

Just for Me

Can you relate to the woman I have described? Have you set aside just a few minutes to regain your bearings and restore your joy?

Too often the most important aspect of our lives gets squeezed out when the tyranny of the urgent encroaches. I'd like to challenge you and me to take a fresh look at what's really essential in our lives. If we're genuinely committed to the man in our life, the children who call us "Mom," or the grandchildren who call us "Grandma," then it's imperative to preserve and protect our personal time.

We can't possibly be strong for them if we're not healthy ourselves—physically, emotionally, and spiritually.

So set aside a few minutes each day just for you. If it means getting up before the rest of the family, do it. If it means locking yourself into the bathroom just to ward off the distracters, do it.

Sometimes the telephone, the newspaper, a television program, or a request from one of the kids interrupts your personal time. But don't allow the enemy to rob you of this time with God.

Avoid approaching this time with your own agenda. Create an open, quiet space in your heart for God to come in. Ask Him to show you through His Word exactly what you need.

The Bible is the only book where the Author joins you when you read it. And if you ask Him, the Author will explain its meaning and impact in your life. That's amazing!

Your devotional life can become one of the most valued and treasured parts of your day.

HIS WORD

"Acknowledge and take to heart this day that the LORD is God in heaven above and on the earth below. There is no other" (Deuteronomy 4:39).

MY PART

Seek God, not just with a few minutes of your day, but with your whole heart all day long. He will satisfy and bless you more deeply than ever before. Walking daily with God's direction and control gives great security and satisfaction. You will find your life more productive than you could possibly imagine.

MY STUDY

Psalm 27:7,8;
Luke 2:19,20

"**D**o unto others as you would have them do unto you."

Remember that verse from Sunday school? Unfortunately that statement, the Golden Rule, has almost been forgotten.

The Golden Rule

You know how you feel when you go to a restaurant and receive rude treatment from the waiter. You know what it's like to get cut off in traffic or have someone behind the counter bark orders at you.

Who wouldn't want the world to be a kinder place? But how do we get there?

It sounds impossible until we remember that the Golden Rule was God's idea in the first place. And we know that, with Him, nothing is impossible. It is His will that we treat others as we would have them treat us. He is the One who can empower us, by His Holy Spirit, to live that out in our daily lives.

Let me challenge you to put Him to the test. Ask God to help you put others' needs before your own today and every day. Pay close attention to your behavior and how you respond to those you encounter. When you fall short, confess that to the Lord and ask Him once again to fill you with His Spirit and empower you to live by the Golden Rule.

When you find yourself being unusually kind and sensitive, be sure to give Him the credit. Thank God for what He is doing in you and through you.

Much emotional energy is wasted when we feel frustrated by someone who has violated us, and we can become discouraged by feelings of resentment or bitterness we may have toward someone. It sounds pretty inviting to replace those feelings with kind and gracious thoughts. It makes me know that when I do unto others as I would have them do unto me, it is not only good for them, God is at work in me.

HIS WORD

"In everything, do to others what you would have them do to you, for this sums up the Law and the Prophets" (Matthew 7:12).

MY PART

"Lord Jesus, you know that I cannot put others before myself in my own power. It's impossible. But I want to do what you've asked me to do. Give me the ability today to put others' interest and needs before my own. In Your powerful name, amen."

MY STUDY

Leviticus 25:35–37; Proverbs 22:9

DAY 65

A few years ago, a friend of mine was riding the public transit system in the former Soviet Union. When Jo Anne reached her destination, she got off the train and almost tripped over a man lying on the walkway. At first glance, she thought he had passed out from a long night of drinking.

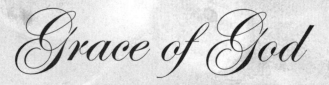

Then she took a closer look. His arms and legs were mangled. He was dead. It appeared he'd fallen stone drunk in front of the train.

Jo Anne did some heavy reflecting that morning. *What would his life have been like had he known Jesus? What would my life be like if I didn't know the Lord?*

She began to see this man from a much different perspective. Without God, she could have been on that sidewalk. *There, but for the grace of God, go I,* she thought. Without the hope of Jesus, Jo Anne knew she could have turned to alcohol and even suicide to relieve the pain of hopelessness.

Most Americans still want to believe that happiness is found in a bigger paycheck or living in a better neighborhood. Yet, hopelessness is running rampant in our country. Despair is not unique to the former Soviet Union. In our nation, it's the byproduct of abundance and godlessness.

Those of us who are privileged to know God's love and forgiveness must spread the word. So often, all it takes to introduce someone to Christ is to tell the story of what God has done for you. Sharing your faith takes only a little thought and preparation. You may be surprised how easy it is.

Men and women all around us are as desperate as that man on the street. If you know Jesus Christ, you have the answer. If you tell just one person today, God can use you to rescue one life from heartbreak.

HIS WORD
"The LORD gives sight to the blind, the LORD lifts up those who are bowed down, the LORD loves the righteous" (Psalm 146:8).

MY PART
Take time before the end of the day to ask yourself the question, "What would my life be like if I didn't know the Lord?" Then pray that God will lead you to someone who needs to hear your answer. You'll be delighted to see what comes your way!

MY STUDY
*Isaiah 38:17;
1 John 4:10*

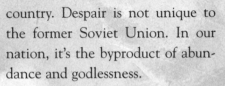

DAY 66

"Sticks and stones may break my bones, but words will never hurt me." Oh, really? Words *can* hurt. In fact cynical comments or derogatory remarks are tough to put out of your mind. Words can cause irreparable damage.

Throwing Stones

We've all been there, standing in a group of friends when the conversation, in just a matter of seconds, shifts to a person who's not there. The gossip and criticism begin. At that moment, we may try to change the subject, but often we put in our perspective or just stand back and listen.

Perhaps you're at a social gathering when you get cornered by someone you consider dull. Wanting to be with your friends instead, you feel stuck. As you're listening to this person, you're looking over her shoulder —eager to begin a conversation with someone else. Those are *thought stones.*

Perhaps you're walking down the street and bump into a neighbor who doesn't quite meet your standards. Without saying a word, your face tells the whole story; disapproval comes through loud and clear. Those are *action stones.*

Now, let's look at a familiar scene recorded in the New Testament. A group of self-righteous cynics had captured an adulterous woman and brought her before Jesus. These Pharisees are ready to throw sticks and stones, and they want Jesus to do the same!

Instead, He showed compassion and forgiveness. Quickly turning the focus back on her accusers, Jesus said, "If any one of you is without sin, let him be the first to throw a stone at her" (John 8:7). In the silent moments that followed, you could hear the rocks drop onto the dirt.

Wouldn't you say it's about time we drop the stones, too? Those stone-shaped *words* are irretrievable. Those stone-shaped *thoughts* are sinful. And those stone-shaped *actions* are shameful. Dear friend, because God desires us to edify one another, there's no doubt His Spirit will empower us to do so.

HIS WORD
"You shall not give false testimony against your neighbor" (Exodus 20:16).

MY PART
"Holy God, please forgive me for the stones I have tossed and for the damage they have caused. Help me to be more cautious and considerate toward others with my words, thoughts, and actions so I may be a blessing to others. Amen."

MY STUDY
Proverbs 10:19; Matthew 12:34–37

DAY 67

You may remember a novel a few years ago that caught the attention of many women.

Fact and Fantasy

The story was about an Iowa farm wife who falls madly in love with a traveling photographer. Their steamy love affair lasted only four days. But for both of them, the passion was more intense than anything they'd ever experienced.

After his four-day photo assignment was over, he begged her to run away with him. She decided not to. She sacrificed what she felt was true love for the sake of her family. Then she regretted her decision for the rest of her life, nursing the longing to run away with her passions and follow her heart.

This story, which captured the imagination of women all across America, begs these questions: What's so compelling about a story of betrayal and adultery? Is the monogamous life really that dull?

The theme of the movie is nothing more than a modern woman's fantasy. An illusion. A daydream. By entering into this fictitious scene, a woman can momentarily escape her own real problems. For a few hours, she can pretend her life is different.

The problem with escape is that the reality of life doesn't change. After finishing a novel, your husband doesn't turn into a handsome, sensitive movie star, and the kids don't quit fighting. The roof still leaks, and the car won't start. Life continues.

Look carefully and honestly at life. There's nothing spectacular about a four-day illicit love affair. It will tear your home apart! No relationship sustains that kind of intensity over time. So don't be looking over your partner's shoulder, hoping someone more exciting will come along. And if you're single, don't believe you need to compromise your standards to find excitement in your life.

Dear friend, the life God will give you will be much more exciting than any romance novel. And it will be real!

HIS WORD

"His divine power has given us . . . very great and precious promises, so that through them you may participate in the divine nature and escape the corruption in the world caused by evil desires"
(2 Peter 1:3,4).

MY PART

If you're looking for passion—and a love relationship that will endure—invest your life in the one you love. Give yourself completely to that person with whom you share a lifelong commitment. Let God build that relationship, and you will experience a love you never could have imagined.

MY STUDY

Genesis 2:21–25;
Proverbs 17:1

Everyone in the world is looking for happiness. I'm convinced the reason so many people come up empty-handed in their search for happiness is that they've never discovered the joy of servanthood.

Finding Happiness

You see, so many people are self-centered that they fail to realize that real satisfaction comes from helping others—reaching out, instead of taking in. Jesus said, "It is more blessed to give than to receive" (Acts 20:35).

My friend Judy spent a summer in South America. While there, she discovered what made her truly content. Judy traveled throughout Argentina showing the *JESUS* film.

One evening she found herself standing on a dirt road. Children were playing all around her, watching the sun set over the mountains. She began to sing the chorus, "How lovely are the feet of those who bring good news." At that moment, Judy realized what truly satisfies her in the deepest places. That night she wrote these words in her journal:

It's really strange. I am totally content and my spirit is happy but I don't have any of the conveniences of American life. All of the things that I thought made me happy are back home, but for some reason I am content. I am satisfied. Fulfilled. Right here in the middle of Argentina.

Judy learned that contentment comes not from external things, but from knowing she is in God's perfect will, doing what He wants her to do.

Where are you looking for contentment? God has given us some wonderful things to enjoy while we're on earth, but the deepest longings of our soul can be met only by Him. This can happen only when His Spirit reigns in our lives. Then we will be exactly where He wants us to be and doing exactly what He wants us to do.

In the center of His will, we will find peace and contentment.

HIS WORD
"Why spend money on what is not bread, and your labor on what does not satisfy? Listen, listen to me, and eat what is good, and your soul will delight in the richest of fare. Give ear and come to me; hear me, that your soul may live"
(Isaiah 55:2,3).

MY PART
Genuine happiness is found not in self-centeredness, but in walking daily in the Holy Spirit and giving of yourself to God and to others. As you apply these principles, you'll find yourself humming as Judy did, "How lovely are the feet of those who bring good news."

MY STUDY
Psalm 145:17–19; Hebrews 10:5–7

DAY 69

Several years ago, a new man started working in Jane's office. Even though she was married, she was very drawn to him both physically and emotionally. He would ask her questions and engage her in meaningful dialogue. He constantly affirmed her and began to meet many of her emotional needs.

Temptation

Jane said, "I was having teenage feelings all over again. It was like a crush, an infatuation."

How can women have victory over temptation like this?

I think it's imperative to identify the source of the temptation. Jesus said, "The thief comes only to steal and kill and destroy; I have come that they may have life, and have it to the full" (John 10:10).

Jesus is not a killjoy. He wants us to have a full and meaningful life. On the other hand, it's clear that our enemy, the devil, has a diabolical plan.

The Scriptures say, "Test the spirits to see whether they are from God" (1 John 4:1). Jane knew the lustful attraction was not from God. So she embarked on what she called a "21-day experiment."

Every day when the temptations would arise, she'd admit, "Lord, I'm feeling lustful thoughts toward this man, but I refuse to allow lust to take over my life. I choose to be faithful in my marriage. You are the only One who can help me." But the pressure was immense. She said, "Sometimes I'd have to renew my mind fifty times a day."

On the nineteenth day, peace came. By the grace of God, she had won the battle.

Is Satan robbing you of an abundant life? Has he stolen the peace and freedom the Lord has promised? Do you harbor some overwhelming feeling that is displeasing to God?

Dear friend, let God help you. Tell Him your struggles. He is waiting and wanting to help you.

HIS WORD
"Watch and pray so that you will not fall into temptation. The spirit is willing, but the body is weak" (Mark 14:38).

MY PART
Please try your own 21-day experiment to help you deal with a temptation, whether it's lust, a critical spirit, pride, or something else. Your prayer may be as brief as "Lord, help me!" Before you go down a destructive path, give God an opportunity to deliver you from temptation.

MY STUDY
2 Samuel 22:2; Proverbs 4:14,15

There's a wonderful legend in Uganda about believers in that country who had a great commitment to prayer. Each believer chose a favorite spot in the open air for extended times of prayer. No one else would use this quiet place.

When a person went regularly to pray, he inevitably would wear down the grass, making a path to that place. If he stopped going to his place, the grass would grow over the path. Therefore, everyone knew whether or not he was neglecting prayer!

Prayer is such a private matter. No one, except God, really knows the extent of your prayer life. But in Uganda, if someone's path became too overgrown, his friends would ask if there was a reason he wasn't praying more!

External motivation may be important for some, but let me assure you, there are many more reasons to pray. Let me give you four reasons to pray.

1. We're commanded to pray.

2. Prayer strengthens our most important relationship—our relationship with God.

3. Prayer relieves our hearts of anxious thoughts and worries.

4. God answers prayer.

Dear friend, being a Christian is *not* following a formula of religious beliefs. Being a Christian is *not* a list of do's and don'ts. Being a Christian is *not* a schedule of activities that wins us favor with a distant God.

Being a Christian is having a mutual, loving relationship with the holy, almighty God of the universe. It's knowing Him intimately and well. It's growing in our understanding of who He is and what He desires for our lives. It's knowing we're His creation, made to have fellowship with Him.

God is committed to you and desires a relationship with you. Once we realize that, we'll be racing to His side at every moment.

The grass would never grow over our path—the path that leads us to Him.

HIS WORD
"Seek the LORD and His strength; seek His face continually" (1 Chronicles 16:11, NASB).

MY PART
"Heavenly Father, forgive me for not spending more time talking with You. Thank You for desiring to have fellowship with me. Thank You for Your patience with me and care for me. I will endeavor to spend more time with You each day. In Your Son's holy name, amen."

MY STUDY
Psalm 65:2; Mark 6:45,46

DAY 71

What began as the happiest moment in her life quickly became Catherine's deepest valley.

A Season

It wasn't supposed to be this way! Katie was the new baby that she'd always wanted. But within three days of the birth, this first-time mother fell into a deep depression. Normally very cheerful and upbeat, Catherine tried desperately to fight off the nagging feeling of sadness. She found herself crying spontaneously and uncontrollably.

To top it all off, she felt guilty. She thought, *Here I just had this beautiful baby girl and she's absolutely wonderful. And I'm feeling absolutely awful.*

While the doctor assured her that depression was common with childbirth and would pass, his words didn't take away the pain.

She was so weary, she couldn't focus on reading the Bible. So Catherine got creative and listened to the Scriptures on tape. She especially loved the psalms. It was her time with God that sustained Catherine. He became her refuge and her strength.

After six weeks in the valley, most of the depression lifted.

For Catherine, her struggle lasted for just a season. For others, it's a lifelong battle. Statistics show that, in this country, one in four women and one in nine men will suffer from a depressive disorder at some point in their lives.

If you find yourself dealing with depression, realize that you're not alone. Many others have experienced the same thing. You can rest assured in knowing two things. First, God promised to never leave you nor forsake you. He is always with you, to listen, to encourage, and to soothe. Second, many godly men and women find great joy in helping others deal with depression and other emotional issues.

Don't let guilt over your feelings keep you from getting the kind of help that you may need. God wants you to live a joyful life, and He will help you do that.

HIS WORD

"Therefore we do not lose heart. Though outwardly we are wasting away, yet inwardly we are being renewed day by day. For our light and momentary troubles are achieving for us an eternal glory that far outweighs them all" (2 Corinthians 4:16,17).

MY PART

Whatever you're dealing with today, I urge you to find a refuge in God. He's not surprised by anything you're feeling or thinking. He knows right where you are, and He will meet you there. He will comfort you. He will give you strength. Just ask Him.

MY STUDY

Job 23:8–10; Psalm 73:21–26

There are people everywhere! Yet, loneliness has reached epidemic proportions.

Having more people around does nothing to improve our sense of closeness or desire for friendship. In fact, when the neighbors get too close, we just construct a higher, thicker wall!

Friendship

There's no greater cure for loneliness than friendship. And there's no more powerful tool for influencing others for Christ than building relationships.

Recently, I ran across some practical ideas for busy women.

First, make appointments with your friends. It's all too easy to say, "Let's get together for lunch sometime," and then "sometime" never comes. Instead, try setting appointments for a specific time and place.

Then, develop a few friendships that are more informal. Everyone needs someone with whom she can be spontaneous.

Also, take some time to jot a note or e-mail a friend, even if she lives in the same town. It takes less of your time than a phone call and can be read and enjoyed by your friend again and again.

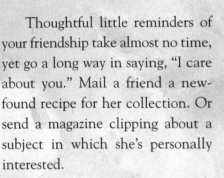

Thoughtful little reminders of your friendship take almost no time, yet go a long way in saying, "I care about you." Mail a friend a new-found recipe for her collection. Or send a magazine clipping about a subject in which she's personally interested.

Set aside a specific time each week and use it to call your friends. Even if you have only thirty minutes, you can call two or three different friends each week and work through your entire circle fairly often.

Don't forget to be faithful with follow-up. When a friend has a problem, write yourself a reminder to call back to see how the situation turned out.

Finally, when you can't be with a friend who's hurting, take time to pray—a wonderful way to offer hope and encouragement.

As God has encouraged you, seek to encourage others and be a blessing.

HIS WORD
"I thank God every time I remember you. In all my prayers for all of you, I always pray with joy because of your partnership in the gospel from the first day until now, being confident of this, that he who began a good work in you will carry it on to completion until the day of Christ Jesus" (Philippians 1:3–6).

MY PART
"Father, help me to invest my time wisely in friendships. Help me to be deliberate and thoughtful about nurturing friendships. Keep me from being passive about this essential aspect of the Christian life. Amen."

MY STUDY
Proverbs 17:17; Ecclesiastes 4:9,10

DAY 73

Some people are never happy. They gripe about everything from the weather to the government. Yet, if we're honest, we'd all have to admit there are times when we're guilty of complaining, too.

Guilty?

Maya Angelou, a poet and author, tells about being reared in Stamps, Arkansas, by her grandmother who owned the local market.

Her grandmother had a routine for whenever people who were known to be complainers entered her store. She'd call Maya to come inside and listen when Brother Thomas would begin complaining about the summer heat. Grandma would wink at Maya.

Then she'd listen to a farmer gripe about his blistered hands and his stubborn pack of mules. Again, Grandma would wink knowingly at little Maya.

When the customers left, she'd say to her granddaughter, "Maya, there are people who went to sleep last night all over the world, poor and rich and white and black, but they will never wake again. And those dead folks would do anything to have just five minutes of this weather or ten minutes of plowing. So, watch yourself about complaining, Maya. *What you're supposed* to do when you don't like a thing is change it. If you can't change it, change the way you think about it. Don't complain."

In the thirteenth psalm, David started with an open admission. He felt as though God had deserted him. There was no denial, no cover up. He was honest with his emotions.

But soon, after a time of focus on God's character, David's attitude began to shift. By the end of the psalm, he was full of praise for God's faithfulness.

What happened? David decided to trust in the goodness of God. His circumstances hadn't changed, but because he chose to think about God's character rather than his own problems, his whole attitude was transformed.

Dear friend, whether or not God changes your circumstances, you can change your attitude.

HIS WORD
"Do everything without complaining or arguing, so that you may become blameless and pure, children of God without fault in a crooked and depraved generation, in which you shine like stars in the universe" (Philippians 2:14,15).

MY PART
Is something bothering you today? If you find yourself tempted to complain, don't. Take your feelings to God and express them to Him. Then, meditate on His character. He is absolutely trustworthy. No circumstances are beyond His control. He cares for you. Resolve to trust Him.

MY STUDY
Job 8:20,21;
Psalm 13:1–6

Karen had a knack for saying the right things in the wrong way. She had a gracious heart, but she could sometimes be abrasive.

Communicating

Others would flinch whenever Karen would offer ideas. If she disagreed, her response would be, "That doesn't make sense at all!" or, "That will never work. Haven't you thought of this or that?"

Even though her observations were valid and her ideas were right, people didn't want to listen.

Karen's roommate, Sallie, saw this happen time and time again. She really wanted to help her friend be less abrasive. So she prayed about what to say and that Karen would be open.

One day, Karen walked in and unexpectedly said, "Sallie, something's wrong. I don't get it. What is it about me that causes people to react whenever I make a suggestion?" That was the golden opportunity for which Sallie had been praying. Karen was ready to listen.

She talked to her about the three M's of communication. First, the *message*—the content must be filled with truth. Second, the *motive*—our intent must be absolutely pure. Third, the *manner*—our style must be filled with grace.

There was no question about Karen's message. Usually, she had the right thing to say. And her motive was good. She wasn't self-promoting. The third one though —her manner—was the problem. Together, the roommates worked on that.

Think of the people in your life —your spouse, your children, your friends, your coworkers. Do they tend to bristle when you speak your mind? Does your input get rejected? At times, do you find your "pearls of wisdom" are ignored?

Practice the three M's of communication and let God's Spirit help you. You'll find your words will have a more godly impact on those around you. People will hear your words and recognize your motive when you say something with grace and love.

HIS WORD

"Let your conversation be always full of grace, seasoned with salt, so that you may know how to answer everyone" (Colossians 4:6).

MY PART

How can we ensure that our speech is seasoned—flavored —with grace? The best way is to allow the Holy Spirit to control our lives. With His help, the fruit of the Spirit will come out: love, joy, peace, patience, kindness, goodness, faithfulness, gentleness, and self-control. These character traits will surface in our speech. Season everything you say with grace.

MY STUDY

Proverbs 22:11,12; Ecclesiastes 10:12

DAY 75

Mary and Martha, the sisters of Lazarus, were tired of waiting. Four days after they had sent a message for Jesus, He finally came to heal their brother. But by then, Lazarus was dead.

Waiting

Jesus raised Lazarus from the dead, displaying His power not only for the sisters, but for all who were present. Mary and Martha found Him worth the wait.

Sometimes for us, the wait is so long that we begin to doubt God's goodness and His power.

That's exactly how Earl and Sandy felt. Their two youngest children were away at college and they enjoyed a nice suburban lifestyle. Earl had a good job as a computer parts manager and his wife worked part-time.

Then, after twenty-eight years of faithful service, Earl was laid off. It was quite a blow to the family, but especially to Earl's self-esteem. He never pictured himself unemployed. Now he was jobless, and without a college degree. The stack of unpaid bills grew daily.

Résumés, interviews, phone calls—the process began and continued for months. Then the months became years. Earl was overqualified for most jobs. He was approaching age fifty-five and getting tired of people asking, "How's the job hunt going?" Finally, right before Christmas of year number three, God provided a job. The wait had ended!

Let me share some valuable lessons Earl learned through waiting. You can remember them with the acrostic WAIT.

W—*Worship*. When waiting, don't lose sight of God's character. His goodness and faithfulness never change.

A—*Attitude*. Guard your attitude. See the situation through God's eyes.

I—*Involvement*. While waiting, stay involved in God's work in the lives of others. This will keep you from withdrawing and wallowing in self-pity.

T—*Training*. Remember, consider this to be a time for training in godliness.

God uses waiting for our benefit. Make the most of these times and know that God is at work.

HIS WORD

"Those who hope in the LORD will renew their strength. They will soar on wings like eagles; they will run and not grow weary, they will walk and not be faint" (Isaiah 40:31).

MY PART

"Almighty God, thank You for giving me times of waiting. I know that You intend them for my benefit, part of the step-by-step process of helping me to become more godly. I will wait patiently for You to bring me through each step. In Jesus' faithful name, amen."

MY STUDY

Psalm 27:14;
1 Corinthians 4:5

Diane had just begun working at a school when the teachers went on strike, and she didn't feel she should participate. Along with a few other teachers, Diane crossed the picket line. The strike was resolved quickly, but the impact lingered.

Cindy's Heart

The gym teacher, Cindy, was tough and loud. Because Diane had crossed the picket line, Cindy had it in for Diane and did everything to make her life miserable. Cindy would humiliate and degrade her in front of the other teachers. Naturally, Diane wanted to avoid Cindy, but she knew that was not what God wanted.

So Diane looked for ways to be kind. Cindy was surprised when Diane inquired about her health after an illness. Over time, Cindy's anger lessened, and little by little, she softened.

One day, Cindy asked Diane if they could talk. She began crying as she told Diane about several personal problems. Cindy said, "Diane, everybody thinks that I'm really tough because I put up this front. I'm not. I'm just like everyone else." Diane gave her a hug and told her that she would be praying for her.

After a few years, Diane resigned from the school to join the staff of Campus Crusade for Christ. While Diane learned to share her faith, Cindy kept coming back to mind. So Diane wrote to her and enclosed a booklet called the *Four Spiritual Laws*, which explains how someone can know God personally. Cindy wrote back right away, saying only that she'd read the booklet. But God was working on Cindy's heart.

Six months later, Cindy wrote to Diane again, saying, "Diane, I've been dating John. For Christmas, he gave me a Bible, sat me down, and shared the gospel with me. I accepted Christ!"

Diane had planted seeds in Cindy's life, and God used her faithfulness to work on Cindy's heart. My friends, be faithful to share Christ with others.

HIS WORD

"*Then I heard the voice of the Lord saying, 'Whom shall I send? And who will go for us?' And I said, 'Here am I. Send me!'*" (Isaiah 6:8).

MY PART

Look for opportunities to demonstrate God's love and concern for someone who is not so easy to love. Share the good news with that person. Like Diane, you'll be amazed at how God can use you to influence your friend's life for Him.

MY STUDY

Psalm 96:2,3; Mark 5:18–20

DAY 77

Richard and Nancy were newly-weds and new believers. One night they had an argument. The longer it went on, the more Richard persuaded himself that he was right and Nancy was wrong.

Resolution

As Richard walked into another room, a verse came to him: "Do not let the sun go down while you are still angry" (Ephesians 4:26). Richard thought, *Boy, am I glad it's already nighttime. I can be angry 'til tomorrow!*

That's what I call "accommodating theology"!

Scripture is clear that we're not to coddle and nurture feelings of anger. We're to work toward *resolution*, quickly and with love.

God knows that unresolved anger festers and turns into bitterness. Paul said that holding onto anger will "give the devil a foothold" (Ephesians 4:27).

Picture the enemy climbing an icy mountain. All the devil can do is slide down unless there's a notch to grab. Bitterness provides that place. And once he's latched on, he does not easily let go. As a result, individuals, marriages, churches, and even nations are destroyed by unresolved anger.

You have a choice in how you will respond to people and to problems. You can choose to respond with humility and love or you can choose to respond in anger.

Ultimately, you need to remember how Jesus Christ has loved and forgiven you. Each one of us has given God countless reasons to be angry. Yet He continually extends His mercy to us.

Are you struggling with unresolved anger today? Don't let it continue, giving the enemy a foothold! Humble yourself before God and before the person with whom you are angry. It won't be easy. But you can't accept the free gift of God's grace without recognizing your obligation to let go of your own anger.

When you deal righteously with your anger, you will be at peace with yourself, at peace with others, and at peace with God.

HIS WORD

"You used to walk in these ways, in the life you once lived. But now you must rid yourselves of all such things as these: anger, rage, malice, slander, and filthy language from your lips" (Colossians 3:7,8).

MY PART

You cannot influence your world for Christ when you're angry. Be filled with grace and love. And the only way to truly demonstrate grace and love is to be filled with the Holy Spirit and to allow Him to work through you.

MY STUDY

Proverbs 29:22; Ecclesiastes 7:9

From totally different backgrounds, Tara and Joy became friends during college.

Tara had been to church only a handful of times, whereas Joy had grown up memorizing Scripture and attending church three times a week. But as Joy grew older, she began to have doubts about Christianity.

Seen, Known, Heard

College became a time of spiritual testing for Joy. She found it too difficult to talk about her faith to Tara. She had too many questions and too few answers. Even when they lived together, Joy read her Bible in private and was very vague about where she stood spiritually.

Two years after graduation, Tara visited Joy. Joy was a different person! For the first time Tara heard her talk openly about her relationship with God. She met Joy's parents and Christian friends and attended church with Joy.

At the end of their weekend together, Tara said that she was impressed. "I've seen a lot of hypocrites," she said. "But you guys actually do what you say."

Then Joy explained to Tara, "When I left college, I

felt spiritually bankrupt. But I've come to a fresh understanding of God's love and forgiveness." Tara did not accept Christ from this experience, but she was able to see the difference a relationship with God made in Joy's life. Joy trusts that, in time, she'll be able to introduce Tara to Christ.

Someone has said that to share the gospel effectively, you need to be *seen*, be *known*, and be *heard*.

To be *seen* means that your life must look different because of your relationship with God.

To be *known* involves loving non-Christians—showing genuine interest in their activities and relationships; being transparent; honestly letting them see God working on your weaknesses.

To be *heard* means expressing openly your thanks to God for the gift of salvation.

My friend, let your life draw others to Christ as they see Him in you.

HIS WORD
"*Sing to the LORD, for he has done glorious things; let this be known to all the world*" (Isaiah 12:5).

MY PART
"*Gracious heavenly Father, the people in my life—friends, family, coworkers— are there by Your design. Give me boldness as I allow others to see You working in me. I desire to make a difference for eternity as I am seen, known, and heard. Amen.*"

MY STUDY
Psalm 67:1–3; Acts 1:8

Bonnie, a woman in her mid-thirties, felt stuck in a very difficult work environment. Her boss was a tyrant. Even so, Bonnie didn't feel she could quit her job.

The Blues

In trying to cope, she began to eat. Over a six-month period, she went from size 8 to size 14. Bonnie became very depressed and felt terrible about herself. Then a friend gave her a weekend get-away at a hotel. While there, she tried the exercise machines and discovered that she really enjoyed working out.

So Bonnie began to exercise at home. After four months, Bonnie lost twenty pounds and felt terrific—both physically and emotionally. She gained the courage to quit her job and find a much better one.

Depression is something most people go through at some point in their lives. But while experiencing the blues is part of being a normal human being, we don't have to stay blue.

As Bonnie discovered, exercise can strengthen both the body and the spirit. And there are other simple but effective ways to get beyond mild depression.

First, don't avoid talking to God because you feel you're not worthy. Take everything to the Lord in prayer. He can handle it! Remember that God's love for you is limitless, and He has promised special help for the broken and weary.

Next, don't get stuck in guilt or bitterness about the past. As Paul says, "Forgetting what is behind and straining toward what is ahead, I press on toward the goal to win the prize" (Philippians 3:13,14).

You've heard the old hymn, "Count your blessings, name them one by one." Being grateful for what you have is an excellent remedy for pessimism and self-pity. Inventory all your personal assets and give thanks. Gratitude will always give you a fresh perspective on life.

Finally, help someone else. Caring for someone who is hurting will take your focus off your own pain.

HIS WORD

"*The* LORD *is good to those whose hope is in him, to the one who seeks him*" (Lamentations 3:25).

MY PART

The next time you are feeling blue, take your feelings to the Lord in prayer. Share your heart with Him. Don't focus on sins of the past, but look at how God has blessed you, in the past and in the present. Then, reach out and do something nice for someone around you.

MY STUDY

Psalm 42:11; 1 Peter 1:3

DAY 80

You're in a hurry to get to an appointment, so you hop into the car, speed down the road, then realize, "Now, how do I get there?" You've forgotten your map.

Quiet Time

That's the way it is in the Christian life, isn't it? We rush through each day without paying attention to the map, God's guidebook, the Bible. He's given us a compass to correct our direction. All we need to do is stop and look!

I know it can be a struggle to make time for daily devotions. But spending quality time with the Lord every day is absolutely essential if you expect to grow spiritually. For busy people, quiet times won't just happen. You have to plan them.

Most of us find early mornings work best. In fact, the Bible sets a precedent for that. It's recorded a number of times that Jesus rose early in the morning, went to a quiet place, and prayed to the Father.

Our Lord knows how difficult it can be to take time alone with Him. If you're a mother, perhaps your child's afternoon nap may be the best time, or maybe just be-

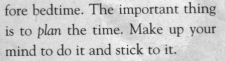

fore bedtime. The important thing is to *plan* the time. Make up your mind to do it and stick to it.

If you don't know what to read, start with a particular book of the Bible. (I suggest the Gospel of Mark or John.) Before you begin reading, pray for the Holy Spirit to teach you. Read a few verses or a chapter. Concentrate on those select lines. Then ask, "What does this passage teach me about God, about myself, about sins to confess or avoid, about commands to obey, about Christian love?"

Keep a notebook or a spiritual journal. Write down what you're learning from each passage. Incorporate what you've discovered into your day. Memorize the verses that are especially meaningful to you.

HIS WORD
"My soul yearns for you in the night; in the morning my spirit longs for you. When your judgments come upon the earth, the people of the world learn righteousness" (Isaiah 26:9).

MY PART
As you take time to study God's Word—the road map of life—and as you enjoy His love and fellowship, your life, and the lives of those around you, will be revolutionized! Begin today to set aside time for Him. Getting to know God is the greatest essential of life.

MY STUDY
Psalm 119:1,2; 2 Timothy 3:14–17

After a year of trouble in her marriage, Terri went to a male coworker for advice. He responded with sympathy. His concern was innocent at first, but then his interest in her grew. He started complimenting her looks, not understanding how a man could reject her. Before long, his comments became very suggestive.

Standing Firm

It had been so long since a man had been attracted to her, the attention felt wonderful. She even considered it healing.

Eventually, she completely gave in to her feelings for this man. Predictably, her marriage ended—and so did her newfound relationship. Terri was devastated.

Consumed with bitterness and rage, Terri went to her pastor and his wife. Instead of blaming herself or the coworker, she said through clenched teeth, "I asked God for help, and He led me to this man. It's God's fault! He's to blame for what has happened!"

Our human tendency is to find someone else to blame when we've made a mess of things. At times, we place the blame on God. But Scripture says there's no one to blame but ourselves. James 1:14 tells us, "Each one is tempted when, by his own evil desire, he is dragged away and enticed."

Sin begins in the mind with an evil thought, often well-disguised as something respectable. That fantasy promises to bring pleasure, power, or success. It becomes sin when we dwell on the thought and allow it to result in wrong attitudes or actions.

My friend, we all face temptation every day, but we don't have to give in.

The first step to breaking its power is to *take responsibility* for your wrong actions or attitudes. Second, *confess to God* that you are to blame and no one else. Third, *thank Him* for the forgiveness you have through Christ. Finally, *flee from temptation.* Resisting the temptation won't get easier. You must get away from it.

God has the victory over sin, and through Him, we can too.

HIS WORD
"Submit yourselves, then, to God. Resist the devil, and he will flee from you" (James 4:7).

MY PART
"Righteous Savior, thank You for providing me with the power to put to death my sinful desires and to choose what is right. When I follow Your law and obey Your Spirit, I will live a more fulfilled, peaceful, and joyful life. Protect me from yielding to temptation. In Your holy name, amen."

MY STUDY
Joshua 24:15; Proverbs 4:14,15

Rick and Becky wanted to send their children to a Christian school, but there was a shortage of space in the kindergarten class. One of their twins, Heather, took the only opening. Her twin brother, Hart, ended up in public school. Becky prayed for him every day that God would allow him to be a "fragrant aroma of Christ" to the teachers and the children in his class.

Sweet Aroma

Soon, Becky noticed that he hadn't eaten his dessert for several days, and one day Heather questioned him about it. Hart responded, "Well, you know, Heather, when you're trying to talk to God about something, and you give up certain foods so you can talk to God better? Well, that's what I've been doing!"

Becky was shocked that her little boy had been fasting! Later as she tucked him into bed, Hart told his mother he had been fasting so that he could tell Brook about Jesus. Brook was a boy in his class who was continually mean to him. He said, "Mommy, I told Brook Jesus loved him and died for him."

Becky was praying for her children to be a "fragrant

aroma of Christ," and her prayers were being answered!

God delights in His children and in their lives. As we live in close relationship with Him and lovingly speak of Him to others, some will come to faith in Him. To them, we are a sweet fragrance of life, eternal life.

My heart was so touched that a little boy fasted and prayed for another child who seemed to be his enemy. Many times in our society, nonbelievers describe Christians as hateful and mean. Yet, Jesus was the most loving person the world has ever known. And He lives *in us!* He wants us to demonstrate love to those we encounter, to be a sweet aroma to them.

HIS WORD

"We are to God the aroma of Christ among those who are being saved and those who are perishing. To the one we are the smell of death; to the other, the fragrance of life" (2 Corinthians 2:15,16).

MY PART

Pray today that you will be a sweet aroma to those around you. Consider fasting for a day, a week, or however long God leads. Through fasting and prayer, you will deepen your outreach to those who do not know Christ.

MY STUDY

Psalm 36:10; Ezekiel 20:41

The angry customer refused to fill out the form. Pushing the paper over the desk to the clerk, he said, "Look, I've already filled this thing out three times. I'm sorry you people can't get it right, but this time, you do it."

A Right?

The clerk jutted out her chin and pushed the form back. "It wasn't *my* mistake," she said. This battle of wills ended when a supervisor intervened.

Nancy witnessed this heated scenario and thought the customer had overreacted. Yet, all that clerk needed to do was apologize for the inconvenience and take care of the matter for him. Instead, she had to be right.

Those words brought a familiar convicting nudge to Nancy's conscience as though the Lord was saying to her, "What about the times in your marriage, your friendships, when you have to be right, instead of soothing a situation with a soft word?" The Lord brought Nancy face-to-face with one more stronghold in her life: the right to be right.

Christ sometimes calls us to lay down this right. Christ emptied Himself of all rights for our sake. Following Him means we must die to ourselves. Even though we love Christ and desire to be like Him, it is often hard to take on the qualities of meekness and humility.

Our goal is to obey Christ, not gain the upper hand in our relationships. Controlled by the Spirit and not self, we will be "kind and compassionate to one another, forgiving each other, just as in Christ God forgave you." That's how Ephesians 4:32 describes what our behavior and our attitude should be. It's not important that we're in control, but that we demonstrate His love.

Nancy knows it's hard to lay down our rights when we've been offended. We want to wound those who've wounded us. It may be normal and natural, but it is completely unworthy of Christ.

HIS WORD

"How is it to your credit if you receive a beating for doing wrong and endure it? But if you suffer for doing good and you endure it, this is commendable before God (1 Peter 2:20).

MY PART

We are complete in Christ, made whole by His love. Therefore, we follow in His footsteps. He helps us be open and humble when we're hurt, misunderstood, or rejected. Laying down the right to be right makes us more like Christ. And when others see this, they see Him.

MY STUDY
Psalm 125:5,6; Isaiah 57:15

DAY 84

After retiring from the United States Air Force, Colonel Glenn Jones joined forces with Campus Crusade for Christ. He was director of our Military Ministry for several years. Then my husband, Bill, recruited Glenn to work with him in his office.

Eternity

As a military officer, Glenn was a gentleman in every respect. He was a quiet, humble, and honorable man. He loved God and was committed to helping take the gospel message throughout the world. Like my husband, Glenn shared his faith wherever he could.

Once when Glenn was on an airplane, he noticed the perfume a flight attendant was wearing. It was a pleasant fragrance. He thought it might be nice for his wife. So he said to the flight attendant, "May I ask what perfume you're wearing?"

She said, "It's Eternity by Calvin Klein."

Glenn, who was so attuned to God, saw this as an opportunity to share Christ. He asked the attendant, "Have you heard about eternity by Jesus Christ?"

In the moments that followed, Glenn shared with the flight attendant how she could know God personally. And right there, in the aisle of that airplane, at her

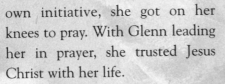

own initiative, she got on her knees to pray. With Glenn leading her in prayer, she trusted Jesus Christ with her life.

That's how Glenn was. He seized any opportunity to open a conversation. Especially if it could lead to a discussion about the gospel.

Sometimes that's the hardest part of sharing our faith, isn't it? Just getting the conversation started. Sometimes, we can simply say, "Hello." Sometimes, we can ask a question. Sometimes, we begin by answering a question. The important part, however, is always being friendly. When you're friendly, others will be, too. When you reach out first, others will respond in like manner. Friendliness is the first step in reaching the hearts of others.

HIS WORD

"The fruit of the righteous is a tree of life, and he who wins souls is wise" (Proverbs 11:30).

MY PART

Are you friendly to others? Do you talk with others at work, at school, or at church? Do you talk with the person standing next to you in line at the grocery store? At the post office? Your child's soccer game? Smile a lot. Initiate a conversation to make the other person feel valued. Seek an opportunity to share Christ.

MY STUDY
Isaiah 6:8;
John 3:13–15

Mary Jane grew up in Birmingham, Alabama, with one objective in mind: to find a handsome husband, create a beautiful home, have adorable children, and accumulate enough money to enjoy life to the fullest.

He Will

She achieved her objective. Her husband was a successful businessman who provided generously for his family. They lived in a lovely home on a lake. They had four darling daughters. Life was very rewarding for them.

There was nothing wrong with her husband, her home, or her children. But there was something wrong with *her*.

In spite of all her blessings, she often felt short-tempered and frustrated. All too often she heard herself getting angry with the children. No matter how often she resolved to quit, her outbreaks of rage kept occurring.

Mary Jane felt increasingly worse about her actions. They were embarrassing to her, and she worried about what she was doing to her little girls.

Although she'd gone to church all her life, it was at a Bible study where she first heard that God wanted to help her. She was desperate for help. She put her faith in Christ and gradually her life began to transform. Her anger subsided.

She realizes now, many years later, that she'd become a new person. She stopped feeling so angry and screaming at her children. She became a better mother, wife, and person. Perhaps the most important change was relief from the anxiety over her own behavior. Today Mary Jane has close relationships with her daughters and their families.

Is there something in your life over which you seem to have no control and want to change? That, my friend, is what Jesus wants to do for you. He wants to change your life!

It sounds almost too good to be true, but it is true. God wants to do away with the old things in your life. He has the power to do it.

HIS WORD

"This is what the Sovereign LORD, the Holy One of Israel, says: 'In repentance and rest is your salvation, in quietness and trust is your strength" (Isaiah 30:15).

MY PART

My friend, God loves you. His plan is for you to be free from hindrances that bind you and hold you back. No matter how hard you try to make yourself better, it never works. Confess your sin to Him. Receive His forgiveness. Invite Him to come into your life and to make you a new creature. He will change your life.

MY STUDY

Proverbs 16:32; Romans 6:6,7

DAY 86

My friend Rebecca was on a mission trip in Russia where she and her team met with Russian teachers. They taught them about Jesus, the Bible, morals, and ethics.

The Internet

Tanya, a Russian teacher of English, told Rebecca, "I knew we would be friends the first time I saw you." In a matter of hours, a wonderful friendship began.

Tanya grew up in communist Russia. Taught by the Orthodox priests in her family, she believed in the existence of God. But that's all.

Today, she knows and believes in His love and forgiveness in her life. Tanya and Rebecca live worlds apart, but computers have kept them connected.

Rebecca has continued helping Tanya grow in her faith through e-mail via the Internet.

In an early correspondence, Rebecca told Tanya about the biblical principles involved in building a trusting friendship. Tanya wrote back with these words, "In this letter you gave me an excellent lesson of friendship and Christianity. I've printed it and keep it in my purse. It helps me to overcome the difficulties of everyday life."

My friend, this really is a beautiful picture of how God works, isn't it?

God has a plan for Tanya's life. In that plan, He sent Rebecca to disciple and encourage Tanya in her faith. Tanya has been very involved in a vital ministry work in her city. She is devoted to sharing her faith. And Tanya's English lessons now have biblical themes. Her family, colleagues, and students are learning about God.

Rebecca's letters are a testimony to Tanya of God's unfailing love. Tanya has put her trust in God, and she's letting Him show her the way to reach others. That's what discipleship is all about. It's coming alongside another person to help her grow in her faith. It's building a relationship on more than external matters, but on the foundation of Christian love.

HIS WORD

"The things you have heard me say in the presence of many witnesses entrust to reliable men who will be qualified to teach others" (2 Timothy 2:2).

MY PART

My friend, let God work in your life. Seize the opportunities He places before you. Use the phone, letters, or the computer to do whatever it takes to communicate God's love to others. You will meet someone today who needs to grow in her faith in Christ. Be ready to disciple her.

MY STUDY

Ezra 7:10; Psalm 89:1,2

On the south coast of China is the city of Macau. Established hundreds of years ago by Portuguese colonists, it's the gateway to China.

Real or Pretend?

Many years ago, import-export businessman John Bowring visited the area. He brought with him a supply of goods from England and Europe.

In those days, there were no electronic communications, so Mr. Bowring and his crew didn't know a typhoon had devastated the island of Macau a few months earlier. They were shocked to see it in utter ruins. But there was one remaining structure: a huge stone Anglican cathedral. Its looming cross, glimmering in the sun, captured their attention.

Mr. Bowring was so moved by the sight of that cross that before he set foot on land, he wrote a hymn we often sing today. Imagine what he saw as he penned these compelling words: "In the cross of Christ I glory, Towering o'er the wrecks of time."

When Mr. Bowring went ashore, he got a closer look at the church! The heavy, hand-carved oak doors were still in place, and the cross was right where he'd seen it from the harbor. But, when he went inside, he found it totally empty. There was absolutely nothing!

Marauders had pillaged and burned the structure. Now, all that remained was the stone facade, just as it stands to this very day!

My friend, I wonder how many of us are like that remarkable structure?

People know we call ourselves "Christians." But if they were able to look *inside* our lives, what would they see? Would there be emptiness?

Like the facade of a movie set, things look real but they're just "pretend." They're fake. They're hollow!

Dear friend, Jesus had strong words for people like that. But He wants you to be genuine in your faith. Let Him change you on the inside and the outside will follow.

HIS WORD

"The lamp of the LORD searches the spirit of a man; it searches out his inmost being" (Proverbs 20:27).

MY PART

Are you feeling "dead" spiritually? You don't have to stay that way. There are three things you can do right now. Pray—talk with God. Ask Him to make you alive. Read—study His Word daily. Spend quality time reading the Bible and allowing God to speak to your heart. Share— talk to another person about the things you're learning as you pray and read.

MY STUDY

Jeremiah 17:10; Romans 7:21–25

DAY 88

Annette felt there had to be more. If she could rate her sense of satisfaction, it was about fifty-fifty. Half of the time, things were manageable and even pleasant. But the other half, life was dull, even awful.

Are You Ready?

Annette was a career woman who liked her job. She was highly skilled and was often applauded for her efforts.

She'd been married for four years to her college sweetheart. Things started out great, but now the honeymoon was over. Reality had struck. She admitted that when he traveled, it was a relief. She'd begun to enjoy time to herself.

Annette thought there just had to be more to life than this. She began to seek spiritual answers. She read a few of Shirley Maclaine's books, read some articles about angels, and even joined a local Bible study. She was a seeker, but not yet a Christian.

One morning, while waiting in an airport, Annette

looked around the terminal and thought to herself, *I wonder if anyone around me knows where to find the answer. And if so, I hope I can sit by them on this flight.*

Sure enough, my friend Sharon ended up in the seat next to Annette. Before long, they were reading through a booklet called *Would You Like to Know God Personally?*

As they reached the end of the flight, Annette understood how she could have a relationship with Christ. She said to Sharon, "I want to open my life to Christ. This is what I've been looking for."

Most of us assume that people don't want anything to do with hearing the gospel. Yet, dear friend, many times their minds are reeling, searching for the answers that will give them purpose, looking for ways to increase their fifty-fifty existence to one that is filled with meaning. They don't know the way. Lead them to the answer—Jesus Christ.

HIS WORD
"Be ready to speak up and tell anyone who asks why you're living the way you are, and always with the utmost courtesy" (1 Peter 3:15, The Message).

MY PART
"Lord Jesus, I encounter people every day who are searching for answers to their problems. Help me to be sensitive to their needs and then be ready to give the answer: that You alone are the way, the truth, and the life. You are the answer. Amen."

MY STUDY
Psalm 40:9,10; Isaiah 43:10–12

friend told me about her pursuit of a "clean slate" in her life. It started when she heard a Christian speaker talk about having a blameless conscience before God and others. That meant dealing with sins of the past.

Battling against pride, she knew what God was calling her to do.

The first visit was with her insurance broker. She'd lied on an application for auto insurance, claiming she drove forty miles a week to work when it was actually 200 miles. She offered to pay him back. He declined the offer but thanked her for her honesty.

Next, she went to her banker. Six months earlier, she had borrowed some money and been untruthful about the purpose of the loan. She confessed and apologized. Amazingly, the banker was sympathetic and didn't take any action against her.

Then came the hardest part. In a college course, she'd cheated on a test by peeking at her Bible to jog her memory. Deep down she knew it was wrong. Even though seven years had passed, she went to the professor—someone she greatly admired —and confessed. It was so embarrassing for her, but the professor was grateful and forgiving.

Perhaps you're thinking, *What's the big deal? Is it really necessary to make things right with people who may not even care?*

Yes. It is. God wants us to reflect His character. In 1 Peter 1:16, God said, "Be holy, because I am holy."

Like my friend, there are times when we have to retrace our steps in order to have a blameless conscience. Believe me, I've been in that position!

Ask God to show you any unconfessed sins. Make a list as the Holy Spirit brings them to mind. Then, seek out those you've offended and ask for their forgiveness. Finally, ask God for His forgiveness. You will find your burden lifted—and few things are more liberating than forgiveness!

HIS WORD

"He who conceals his sins does not prosper, but whoever confesses and renounces them finds mercy" (Proverbs 28:13).

MY PART

Is there someone you've deceived? Perhaps you've been dishonest with your boss about a project on which you're working. Or perhaps you've told your children you would do something you never intended to do. Confess to them and to God. Unburden your heart.

MY STUDY

Job 33:26–28; Luke 5:31,32

DAY 90

Contentment is rare. *Webster's Dictionary* defines the word as "being satisfied with one's possessions, status, or situation." Let me ask you, how often do you feel content?

It seems we are dissatisfied more often than we are content. When you're single, it seems life would be better if you were married. When you're married, it seems life would be sweeter if you had children. And when children are small, it seems life would be simpler if the children were older. And on and on.

But if Paul, having gone through all that he did, could be content in all circumstances, can't we?

If you're dissatisfied with your life, possessions, or position, try these three practical steps to contentment.

First, make a list of what troubles you today. Write down what you do not like about your life.

Second, thank God for each item on your list. Even if you don't necessarily feel thankful, thank God for your situation.

Third, ask God to do whatever is necessary for you to experience His contentment.

When you've taken these three steps, rest and watch Him work. As much as you want to be content, He wants it for you even more.

What's really interesting is this. People in Paul's culture were amazed at the quietness and peace in his soul. When they asked him, "What's your secret?" he talked genuinely about what God had done.

When you learn to be content, others will ask, "What is it about you that's so different?" And God will use the contentment He's given you to reach others with the good news of His salvation.

Choose contentment! Don't fall into the trap of always wanting something better or something different. Don't wait until your life has passed you by to realize that you never got what you really wanted all along—contentment.

HIS WORD
"The LORD will guide you always; he will satisfy your needs in a sun-scorched land and will strengthen your frame. You will be like a well-watered garden, like a spring whose waters never fail" (Isaiah 58:11).

MY PART
"Loving Lord Jesus, forgive me for the times I have been dissatisfied with my life. I know that You are in control. Everything in my life comes from You alone. Help me to cultivate contentment through You. In Your holy name, amen."

MY STUDY
Proverbs 17:15; 1 Timothy 6:7,8

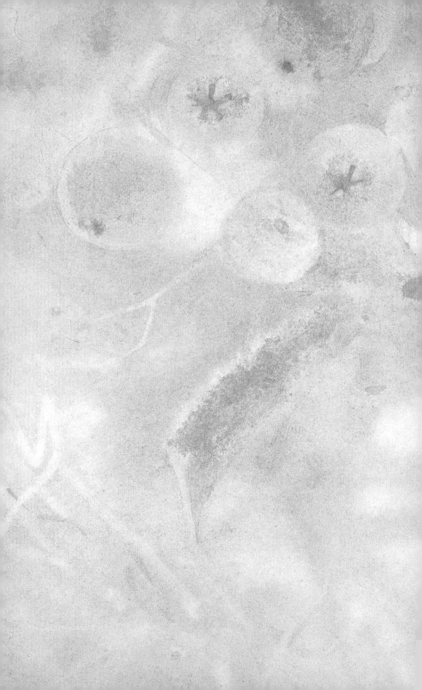

Beginning Your Journey of Joy

These four principles are essential in beginning a journey of joy.

One—God loves you and created you to know Him personally.

God's Love
"God so loved the world that He gave His one and only Son, that whoever believes in Him shall not perish but have eternal life" (John 3:16).

God's Plan
"Now this is eternal life: that they may know you, the only true God, and Jesus Christ, whom you have sent" (John 17:3).

What prevents us from knowing God personally?

Two—People are sinful and separated from God, so we cannot know Him personally or experience His love.

People are Sinful
"All have sinned and fall short of the glory of God" (Romans 3:23).

People were created to have fellowship with God; but, because of our own stubborn self-will, we chose to go our own independent way and fellowship with God was broken. This self-will, characterized by an attitude of active rebellion or passive indifference, is an evidence of what the Bible calls sin.

People are Separated

"The wages of sin is death" [spiritual separation from God] (Romans 6:23).

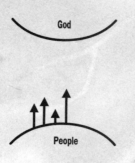

This diagram illustrates that God is holy and people are sinful. A great gulf separates the two. The arrows illustrate that people are continually trying to reach God and establish a personal relationship with Him through our own efforts, such as a good life, philosophy, or religion—but we inevitably fail.

The third principle explains the only way to bridge this gulf…

Three—*Jesus Christ is God's only provision for our sin. Through Him alone we can know God personally and experience His love.*

He Died In Our Place

"God demonstrates His own love toward us, in that while we were yet sinners, Christ died for us" (Romans 5:8).

He Rose from the Dead

"Christ died for our sins...He was buried...He was raised on the third day according to the Scriptures...He appeared to Peter, then to the twelve. After that He appeared to more than five hundred..." (1 Corinthians 15:3–6).

He Is the Only Way to God

"Jesus said to him, 'I am the way, and the truth, and the life; no one comes to the Father but through Me'" (John 14:6).

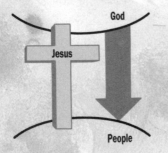

This diagram illustrates that God has bridged the gulf that separates us from Him by sending His Son, Jesus Christ, to die on the cross in our place to pay the penalty for our sins.

It is not enough just to know these three truths...

Four—We must individually receive Jesus Christ as Savior and Lord; then we can know God personally and experience His love.

We Must Receive Christ

"As many as received Him, to them He gave the right to become children of God, even to those who believe in His name" (John 1:12).

We Receive Christ Through Faith

"By grace you have been saved through faith; and that not of yourselves, it is the gift of God; not as a result of works that no one should boast" (Ephesians 2:8,9).

When We Receive Christ, We Experience a New Birth

(Read John 3:1–8.)

We Receive Christ By Personal Invitation

[Christ speaking] "Behold, I stand at the door and knock; if anyone hears My voice and opens the door, I will come in to him" (Revelation 3:20).

Receiving Christ involves turning to God from self (repentance) and trusting Christ to come into our lives to forgive us of our sins and to make us what He wants us to be. Just to agree intellectually that Jesus Christ is the Son of God and that He died on the cross for our sins is not enough. Nor is it enough to have an emotional experience. We receive Jesus Christ by faith, as an act of our will.

These two circles represent two kinds of lives:

Self-Directed Life
S – Self is on the throne
† – Christ is outside the life
• – Interests are directed by self, often resulting in discord and frustration

Christ-Directed Life
† – Christ is in the life and on the throne
S – Self is yielding to Christ
• – Interests are directed by Christ, resulting in harmony with God's plan

Which circle best represents your life?
Which circle would you like to have represent your life?

The following explains how you can receive Christ:

You Can Receive Christ Right Now by Faith Through Prayer
(Prayer is talking with God)

God knows your heart and is not so concerned with your words as He is with the attitude of your heart. The following is a suggested prayer:

> *Lord Jesus, I want to know You personally. Thank You for dying on the cross for my sins. I open the door of my life and receive You as my Savior and Lord. Thank You for forgiving my sins and giving me eternal life. Take control of the throne of my life. Make me the kind of person You want me to be.*

Does this prayer express the desire of your heart?

If it does, I invite you to pray this prayer right now, and Christ will come into your life, as He promised.

How to Know That Christ Is in Your Life

Did you receive Christ into your life? According to His promise in Revelation 3:20, where is Christ right now in relation to you? Christ said that He would come into your life. Would He mislead you? On what authority do you know that God has answered your prayer? (The trustworthiness of God Himself and His Word.)

The Bible Promises Eternal Life to All Who Receive Christ

"The witness is this, that God has given us eternal life, and this life is in His Son. He who has the Son has the life; he who does not have the Son of God does not have the life. These things I have written to you who believe in the name of the Son of God, in order that you may know that you have eternal life" (1 John 5:11–13).

Thank God often that Christ is in your life and that He will never leave you (Hebrews 13:5). You can know on the basis of His promise that Christ lives in you and that you have eternal life from the very moment you invite Him in. He will not deceive you.

An important reminder…

Feelings Can Be Unreliable

You might have expectations about how you should feel after placing your trust in Christ. While feelings are important, they are unreliable indicators of your sincerity or the trustworthiness of God's promise. Our feelings change easily, but God's Word and His character remain constant. This illustration shows the relationship among **fact** (God and His Word), **faith** (our trust in God and His Word), and our **feelings**.

Fact: The chair is strong enough to support you.
Faith: You believe this chair will support you, so you sit in it.

Feeling: You may or may not feel comfortable in this chair, but it continues to support you.

The promise of God's Word, the Bible—not our feelings—is our authority. The Christian lives by faith (trust) in the trustworthiness of God Himself and His Word.

Now That You Have Entered Into a Personal Relationship With Christ

The moment you received Christ by faith, as an act of your will, many things happened, including the following:

- Christ came into your life (Revelation 3:20; Colossians 1:27).
- Your sins were forgiven (Colossians 1:14).
- You became a child of God (John 1:12).
- You received eternal life (John 5:24).
- You began the great adventure for which God created you (John 10:10; 2 Corinthians 5:17; 1 Thessalonians 5:18).

Can you think of anything more wonderful that could happen to you than entering into a personal relationship with Jesus Christ? Would you like to thank God in prayer right now for what He has done for you? By thanking God, you demonstrate your faith.

To enjoy your new relationship with God...

Suggestions for Christian Growth

Spiritual growth results from trusting Jesus Christ. "The righteous man shall live by faith" (Galatians 3:11). A life of faith will enable you to trust God increasingly with every detail of your life, and to practice the following:

G *Go* to God in prayer daily (John 15:7).

R *Read* God's Word daily (Acts 17:11); begin with the Gospel of John.

O *Obey* God moment by moment (John 14:21).

W *Witness* for Christ by your life and words (Matthew 4:19; John 15:8).

T *Trust* God for every detail of your life (1 Peter 5:7).

H *Holy Spirit*—allow Him to control and empower your daily life and witness (Galatians 5:16,17; Acts 1:8; Ephesians 5:18).

Fellowship in a Good Church

God's Word admonishes us not to forsake "the assembling of ourselves together" (Hebrews 10:25). Several logs burn brightly together, but put one aside on the cold hearth and the fire goes out. So it is with your relationship with other Christians. If you do not belong to a church, do not wait to be invited. Take the initiative; call the pastor of a nearby church where Christ is honored and His Word is preached. Start this week, and make plans to attend regularly.

Resources

My Heart in His Hands: Renew a Steadfast Spirit Within Me. Spring—renewal is everywhere; we are reminded to cry out to God, "Renew a steadfast spirit within me." The first of four books in Vonette Bright's new devotional series, this book will give fresh spiritual vision and hope to women of all ages. ISBN 1-56399-161-6

My Heart in His Hands: Set Me Free Indeed. Summer—a time of freedom. Are there bonds that keep you from God's best? With this devotional, a few moments daily can help you draw closer to the One who gives true freedom. This is the second of four in the devotional series. ISBN 1-56399-162-4

My Heart in His Hands: I Delight Greatly in My Lord. Do you stop to appreciate the blessings God has given you? Spend time delighting in God with book three in this devotional series. ISBN 1-56399-163-2

The Joy of Hospitality: Fun Ideas for Evangelistic Entertaining. Co-written with Barbara Ball, this practical book tells how to share your faith through hosting barbecues, coffees, holiday parties, and other events in your home. ISBN 1-56399-057-1

The Joy of Hospitality Cookbook. Filled with uplifting scriptures and quotations, this cookbook contains hundreds of delicious recipes, hospitality tips, sample menus, and family traditions that are sure to make your entertaining a memorable and eternal success. Co-written with Barbara Ball. ISBN 1-56399-077-6

The Greatest Lesson I've Ever Learned. In this treasury of inspiring, real-life experiences, twenty-three prominent women of faith share their "greatest lessons." Does God have faith- and character-building lessons for you in their rich, heart-warming stories? ISBN 1-56399-085-7

Beginning Your Journey of Joy. This adaptation of the *Four Spiritual Laws* speaks in the language of today's women and offers a slightly feminine approach to sharing God's love with your neighbors, friends, and family members. ISBN 1-56399-093-8

These and other fine products from *NewLife* Publications are available from your favorite bookseller or by calling (800) 235-7255 (within U.S.) or (407) 826-2145, or by visiting www.newlifepubs.com.